SCREENSHOT REYKJAVIK

A PHOTOGRAPHIC EXPLORATION

SCOTT SHAW

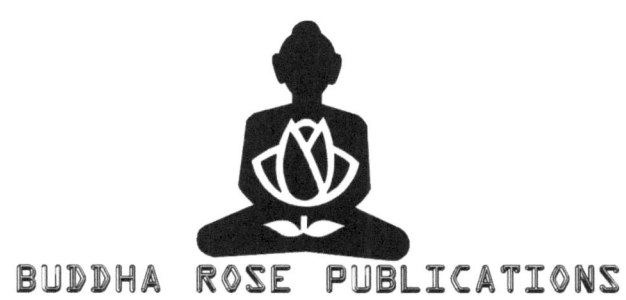

BUDDHA ROSE PUBLICATIONS

Screenshot Reykjavik
A Photographic Exploration
Copyright © 2017 by Scott Shaw
www.scottshaw.com

All Rights Reserved

No part of this publication may be duplicated in any manner without the expressed written permission of the publisher.

First Edition 2017

ISBN: 1-877792-99-3
ISBN: 978-1-877792-99-1

Printed in the United States of America

10 9 8 7 6 5 4 3 2 1

SCREENSHOT REYKJAVIK

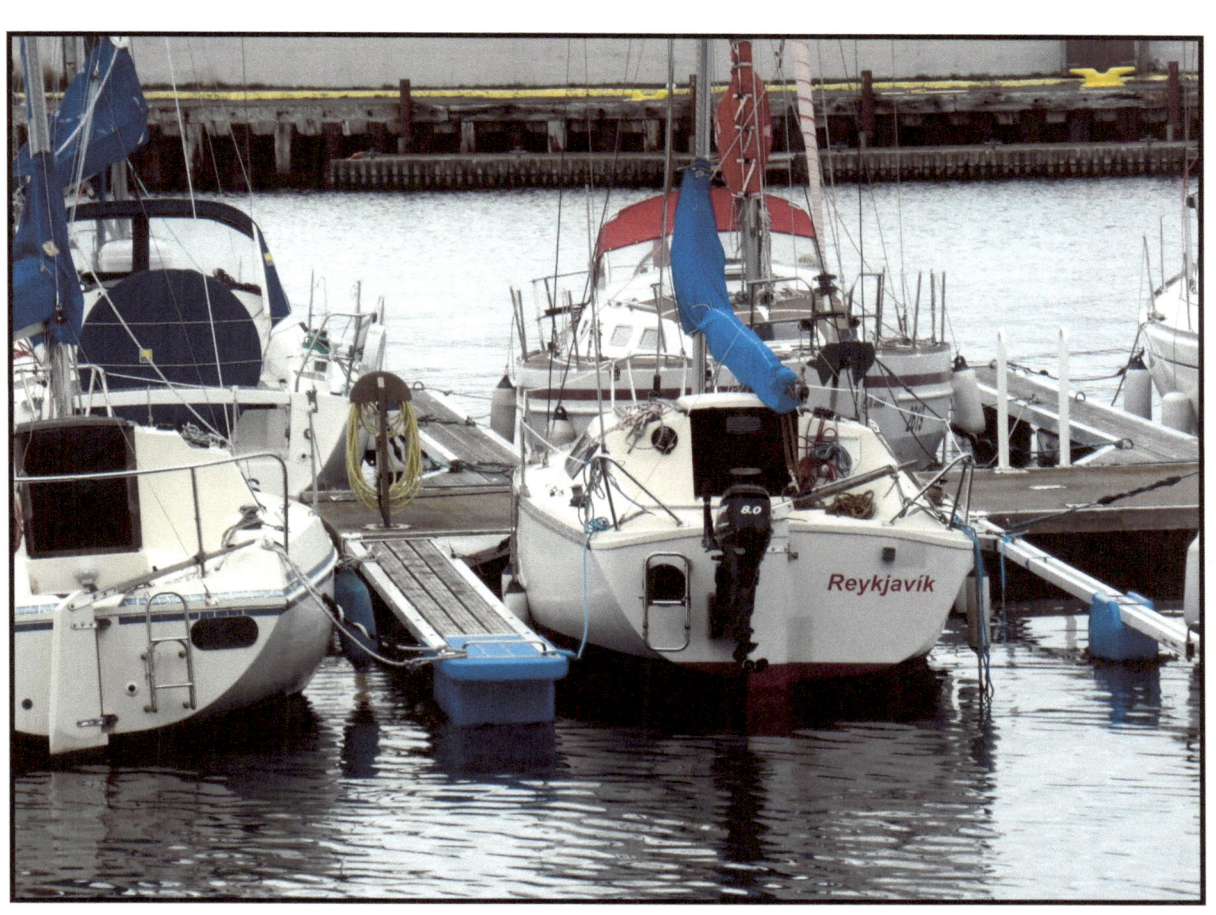

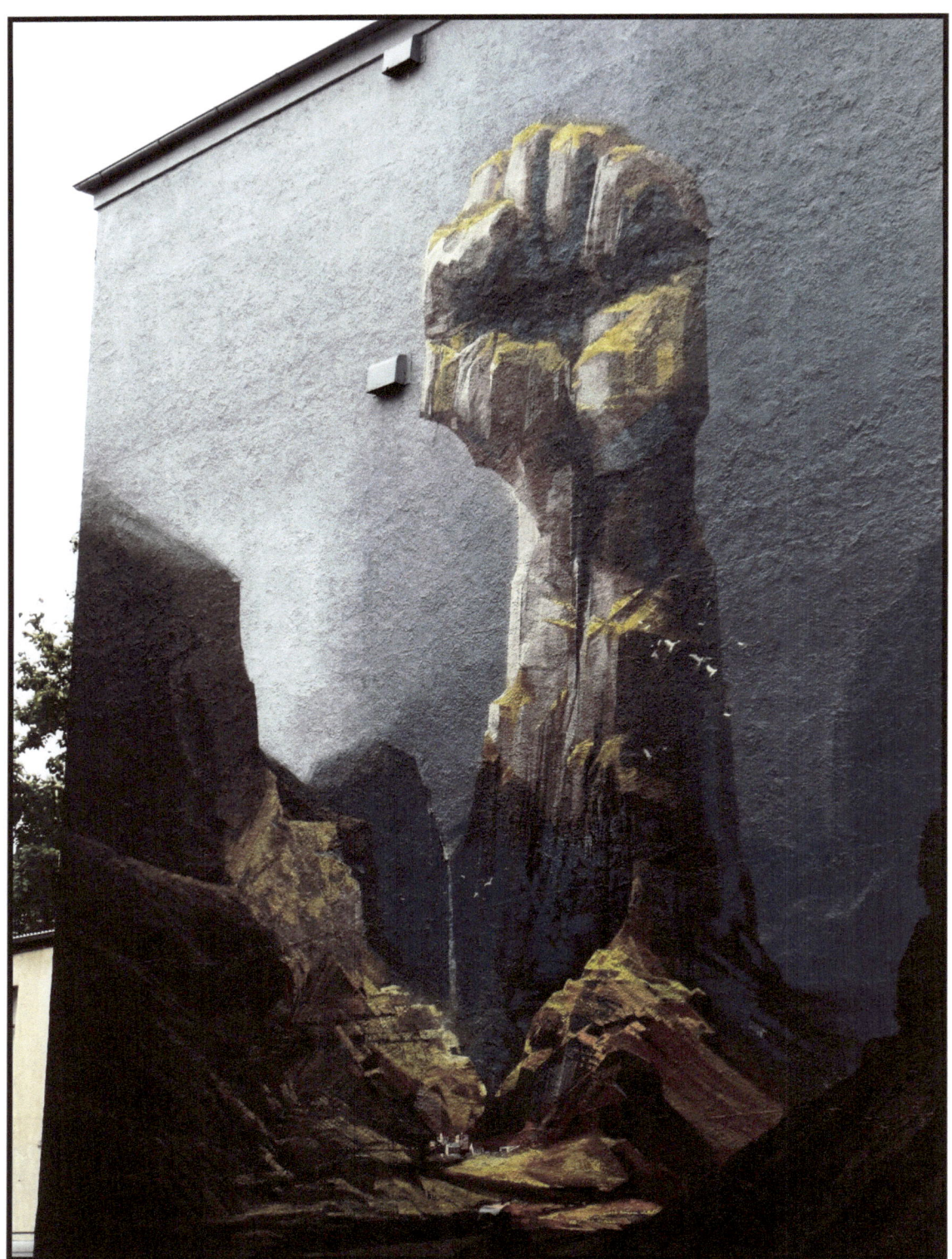

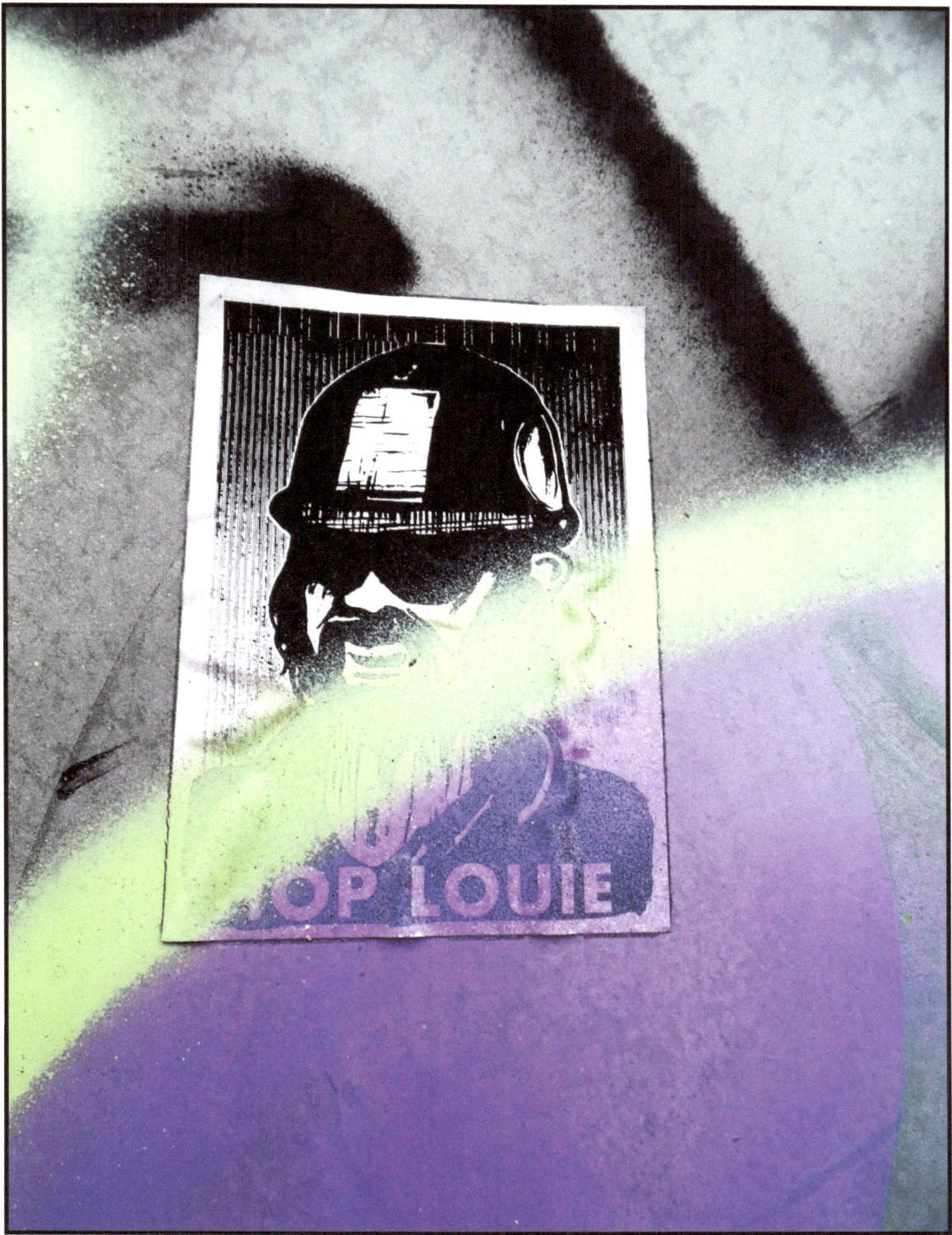

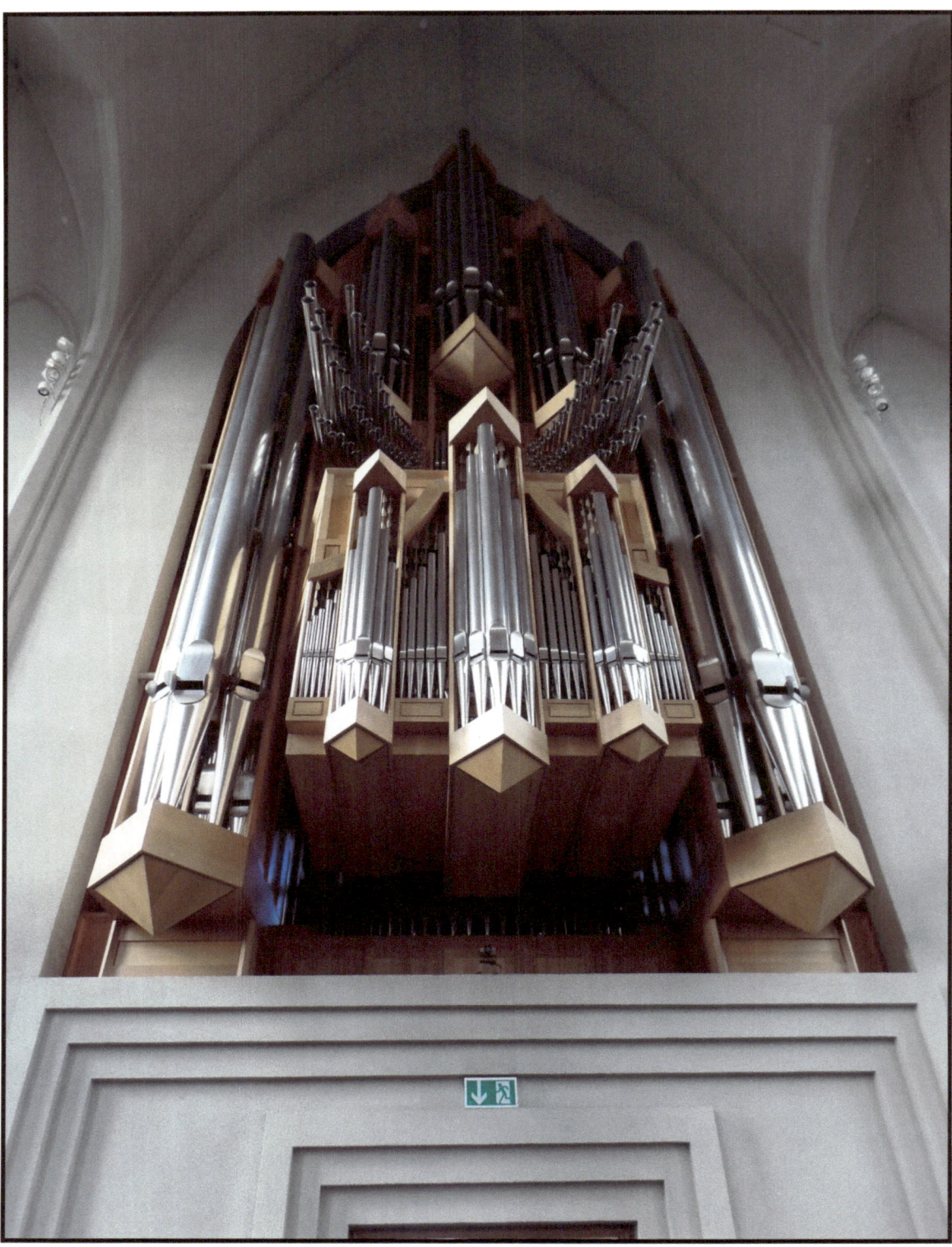

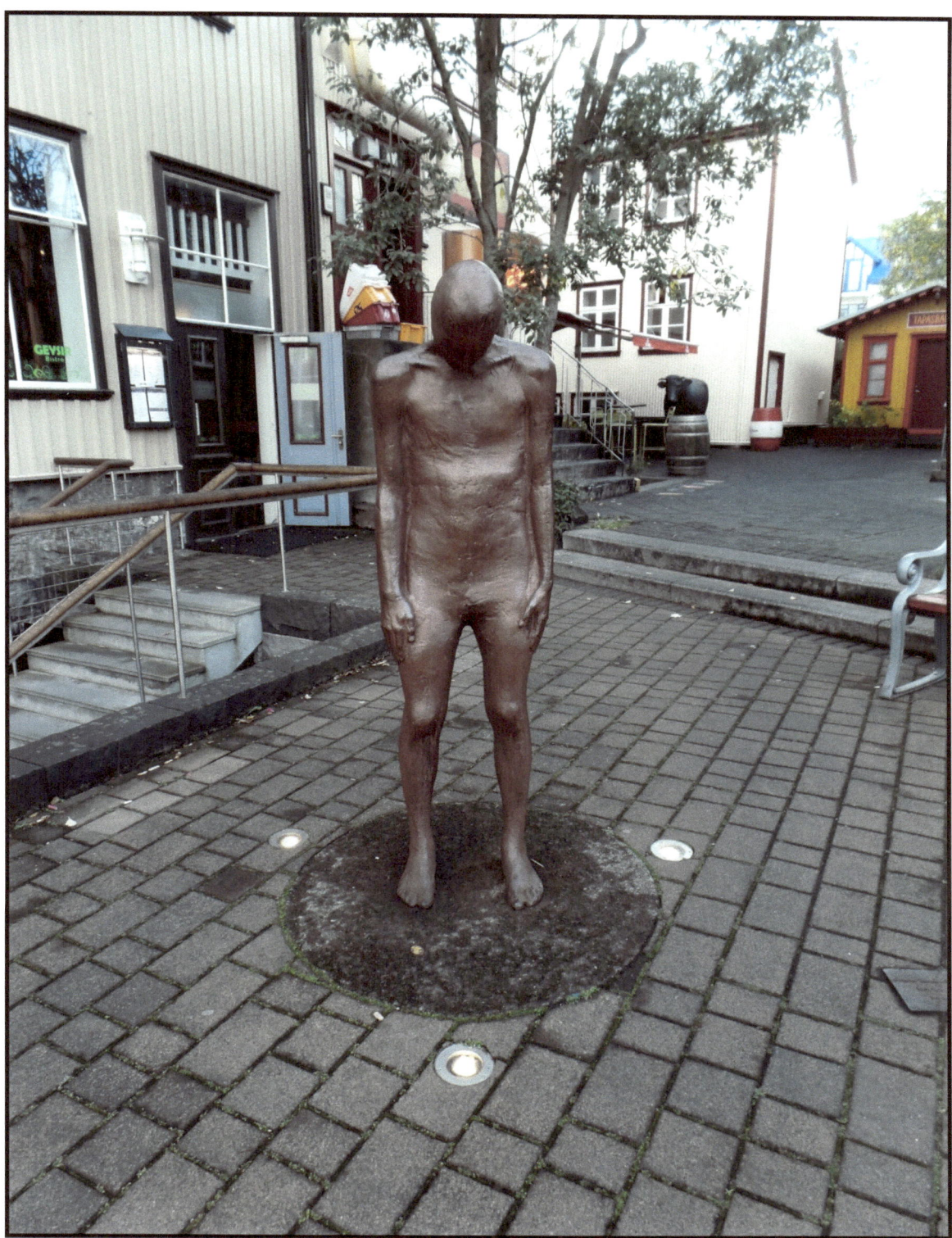

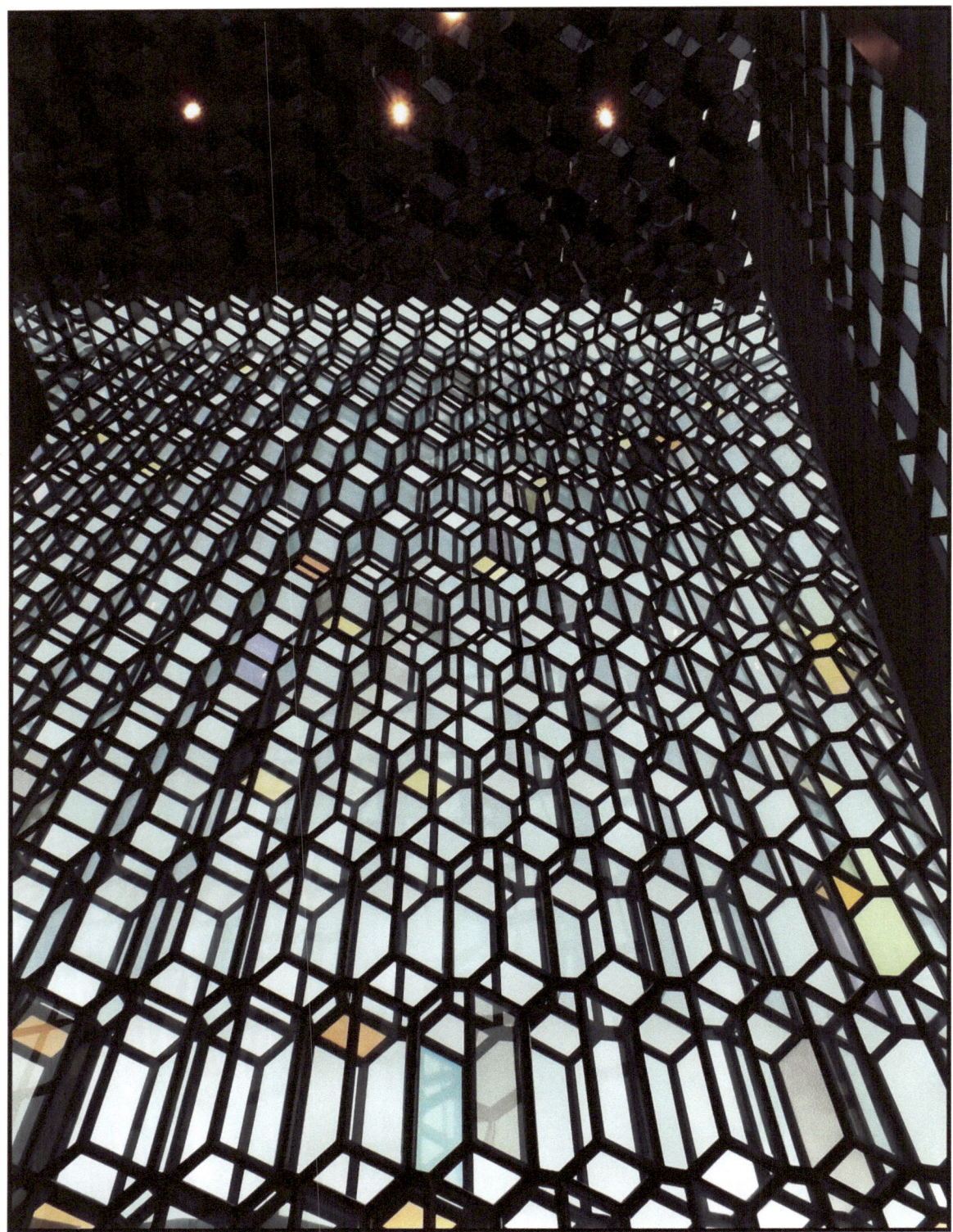

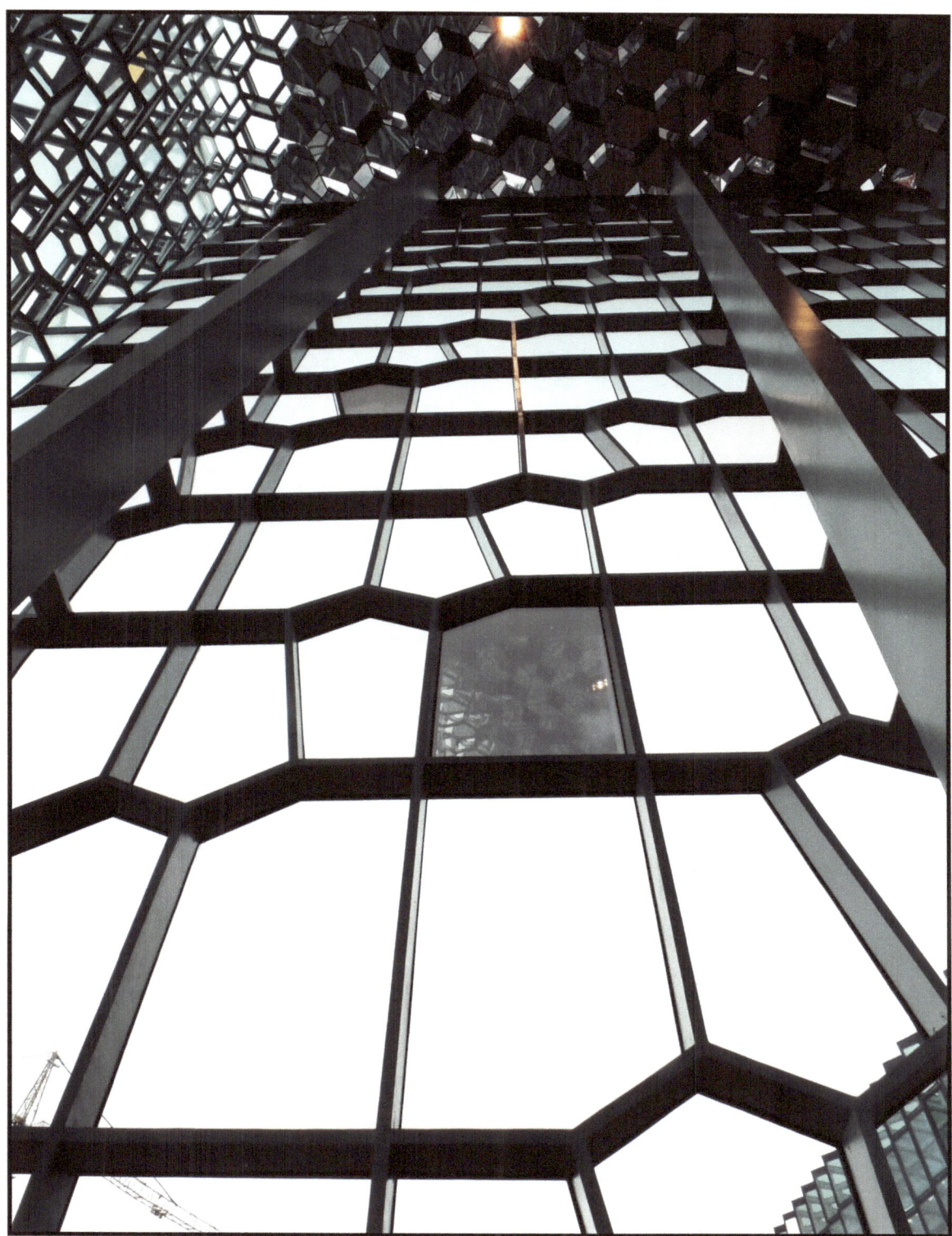

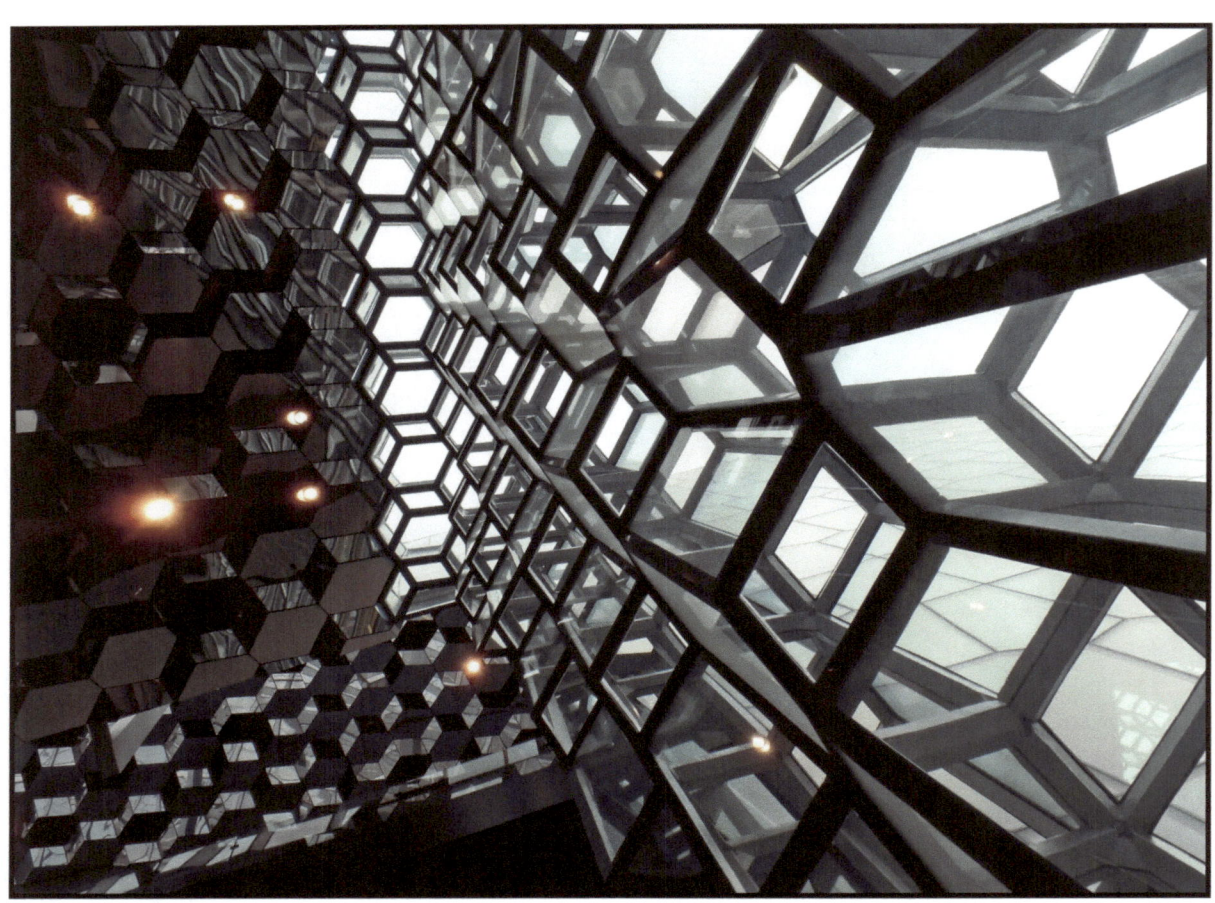

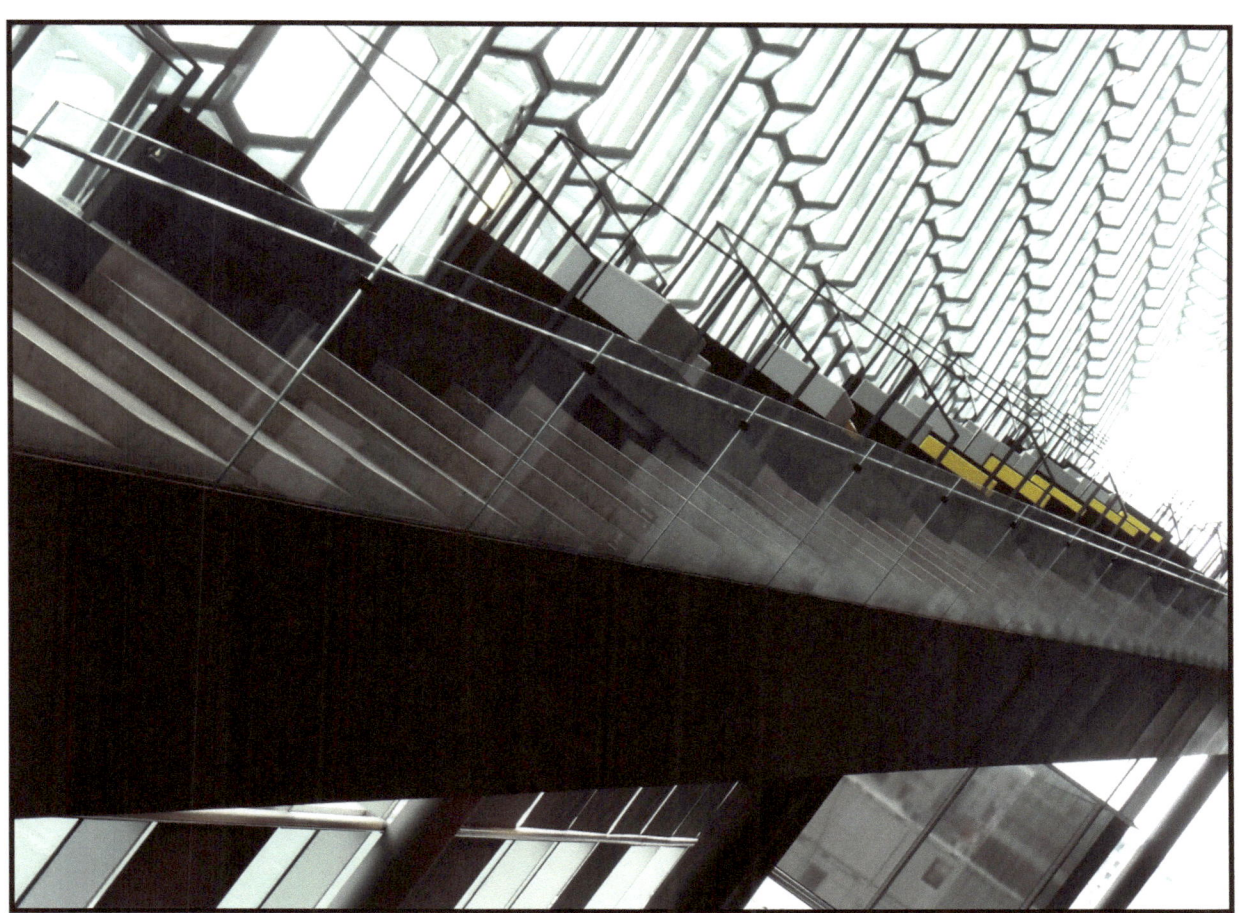

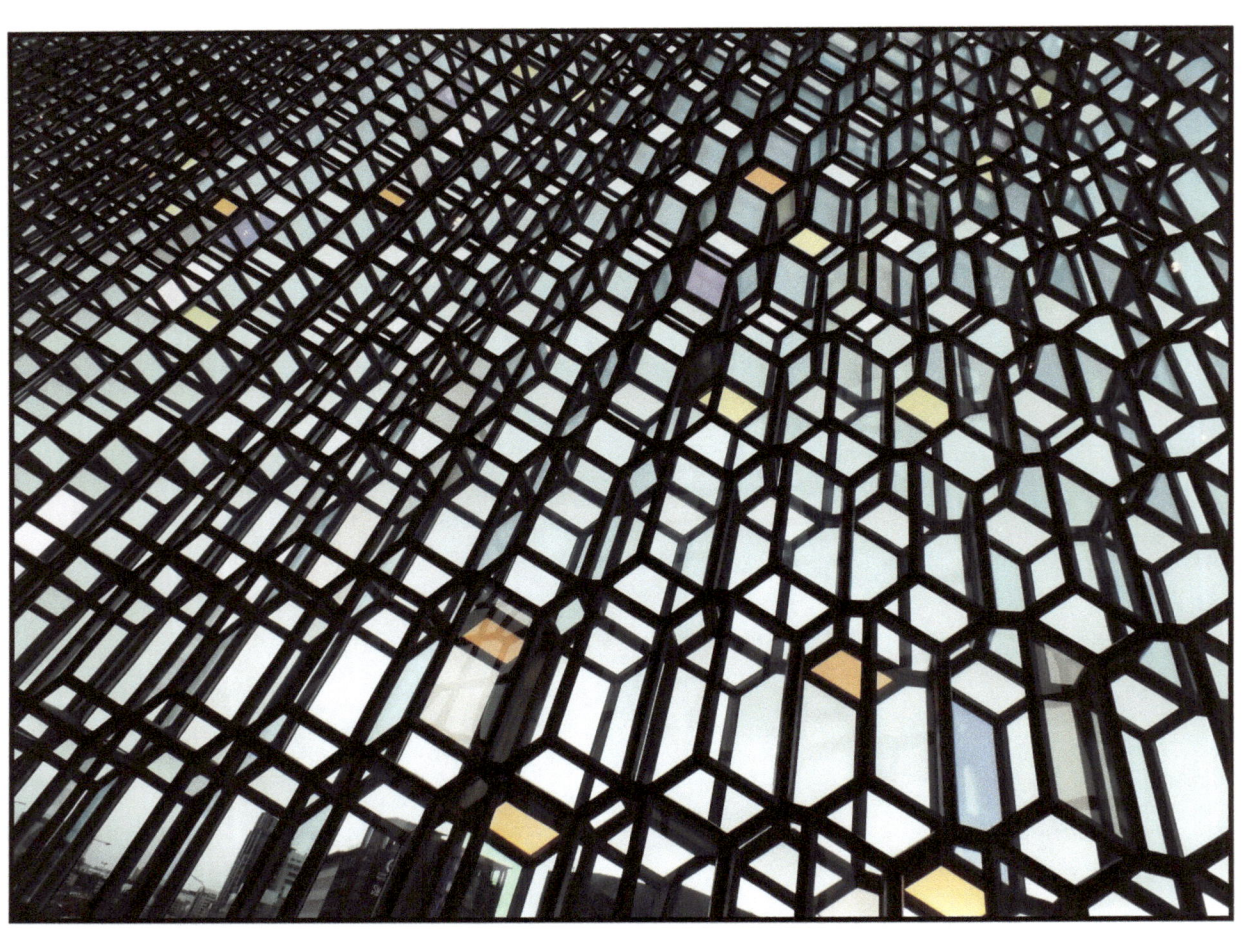

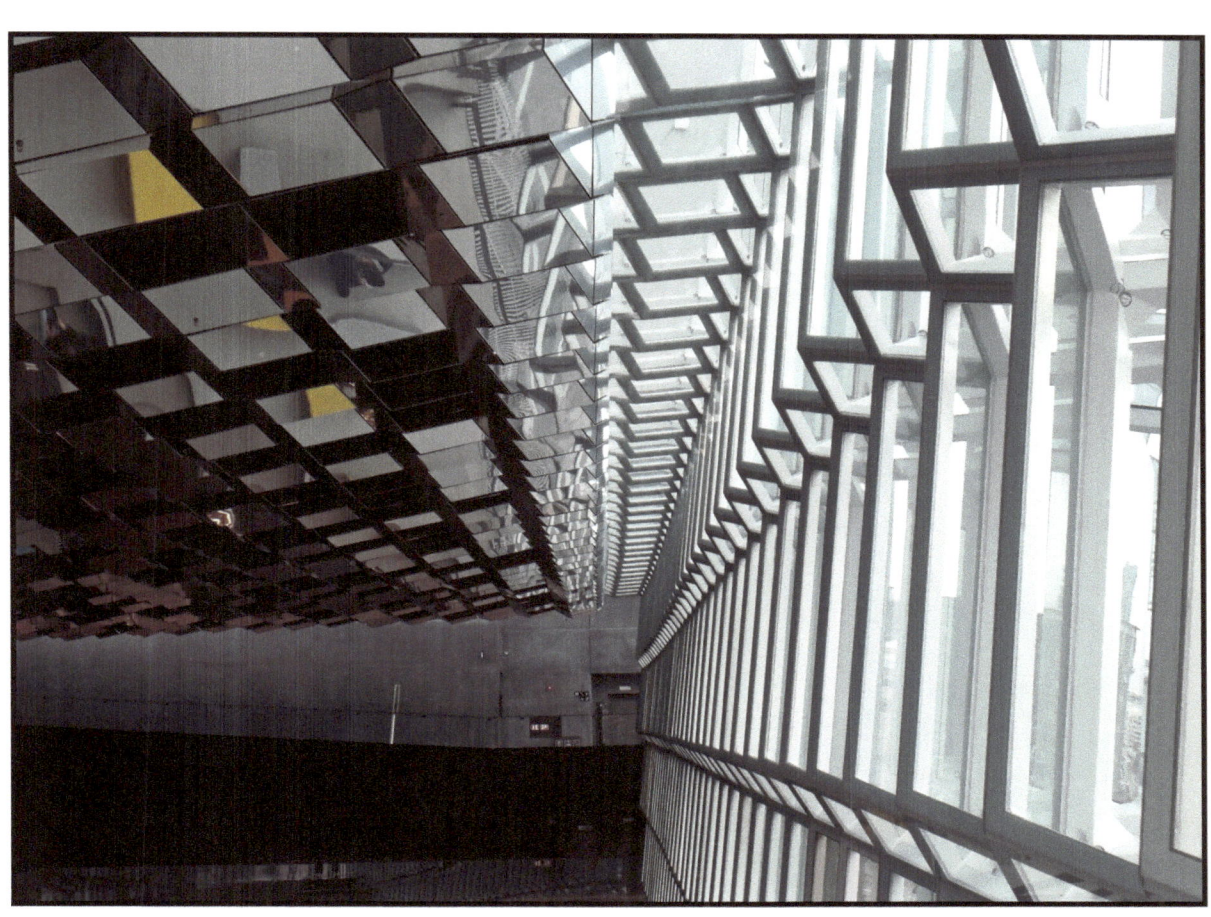

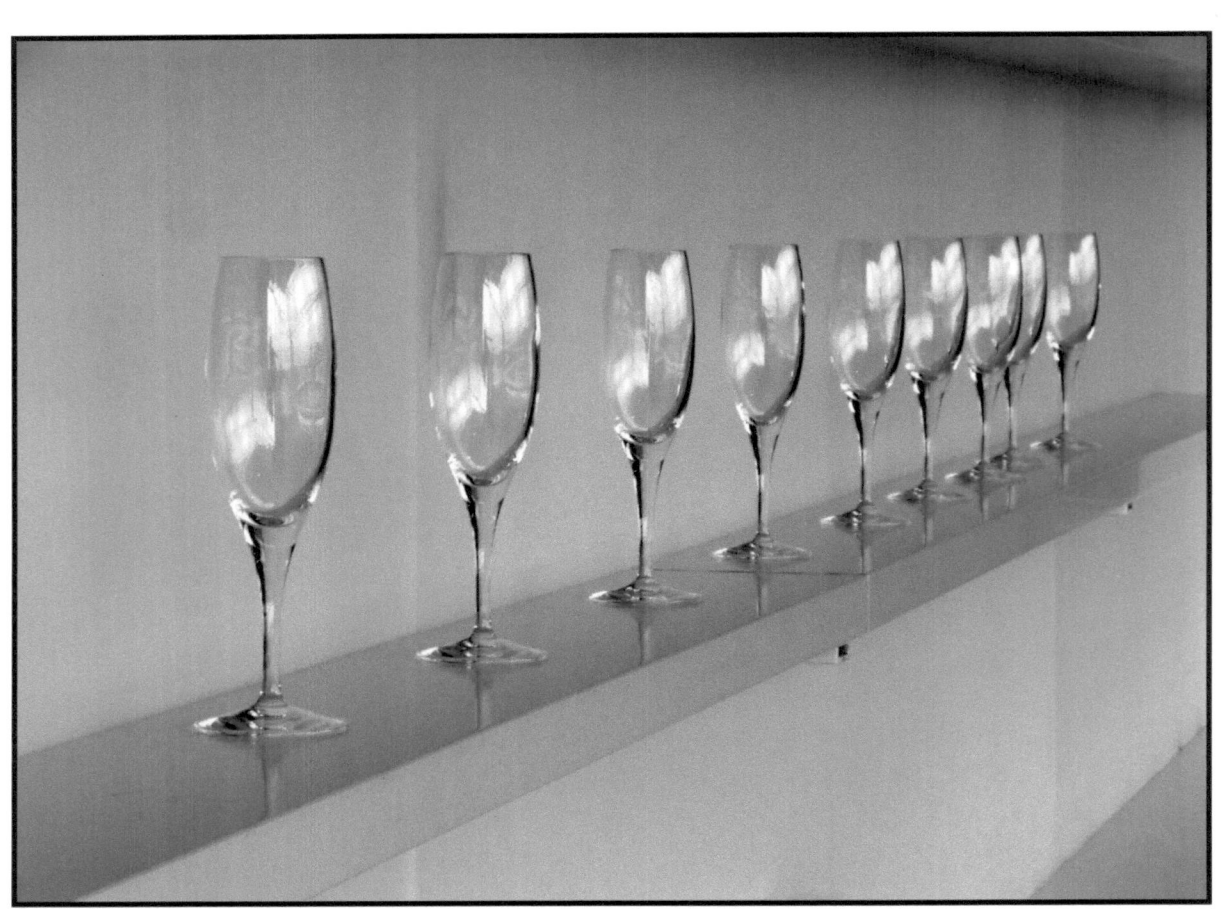

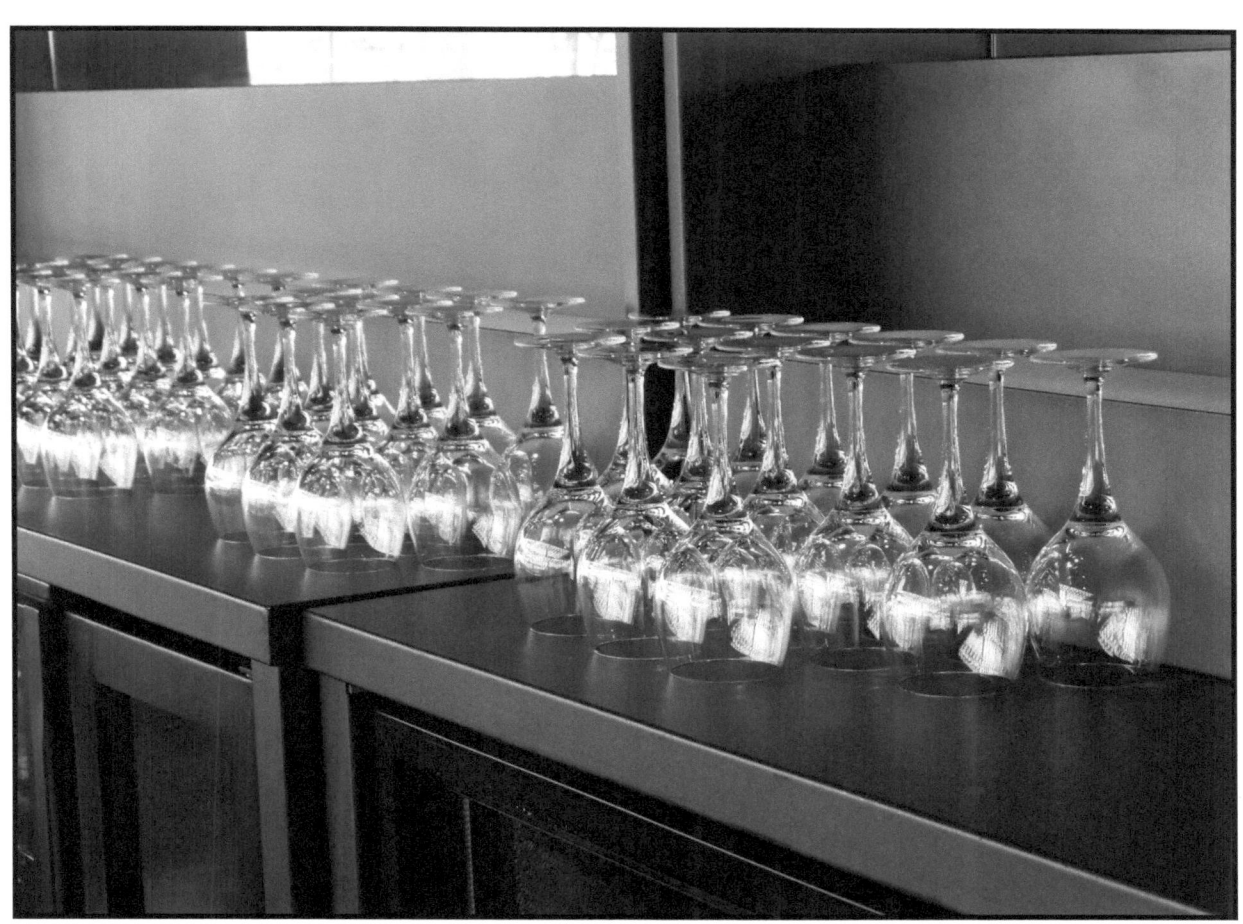

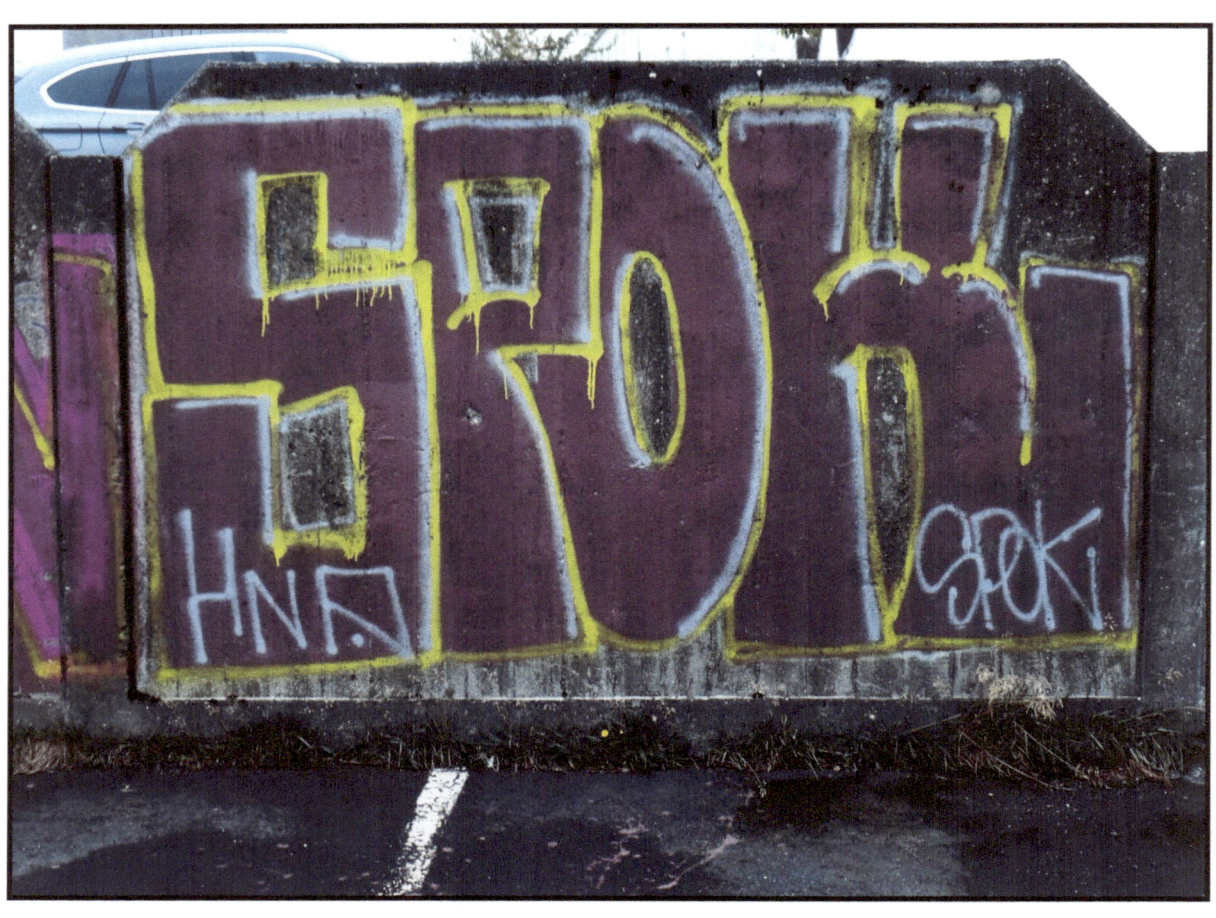

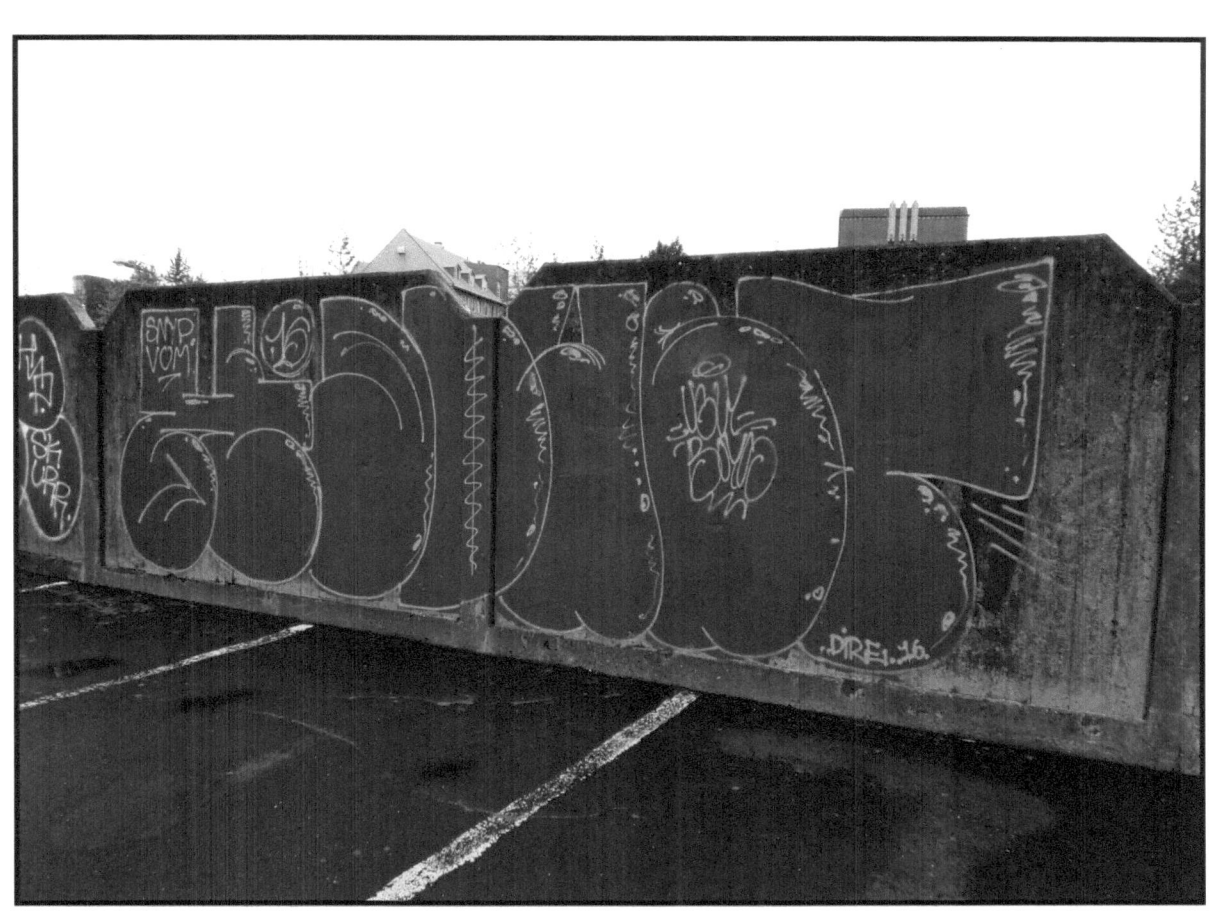

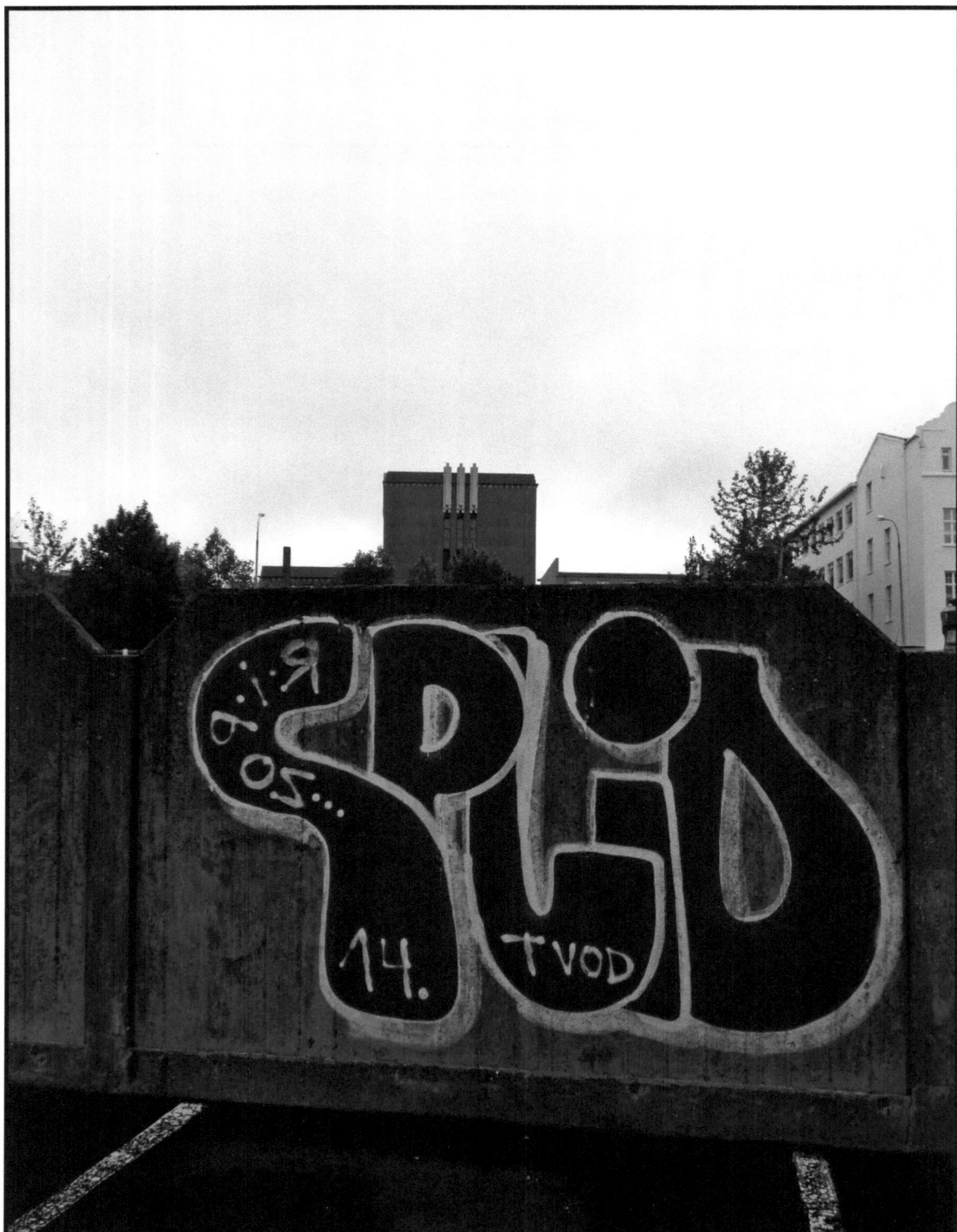

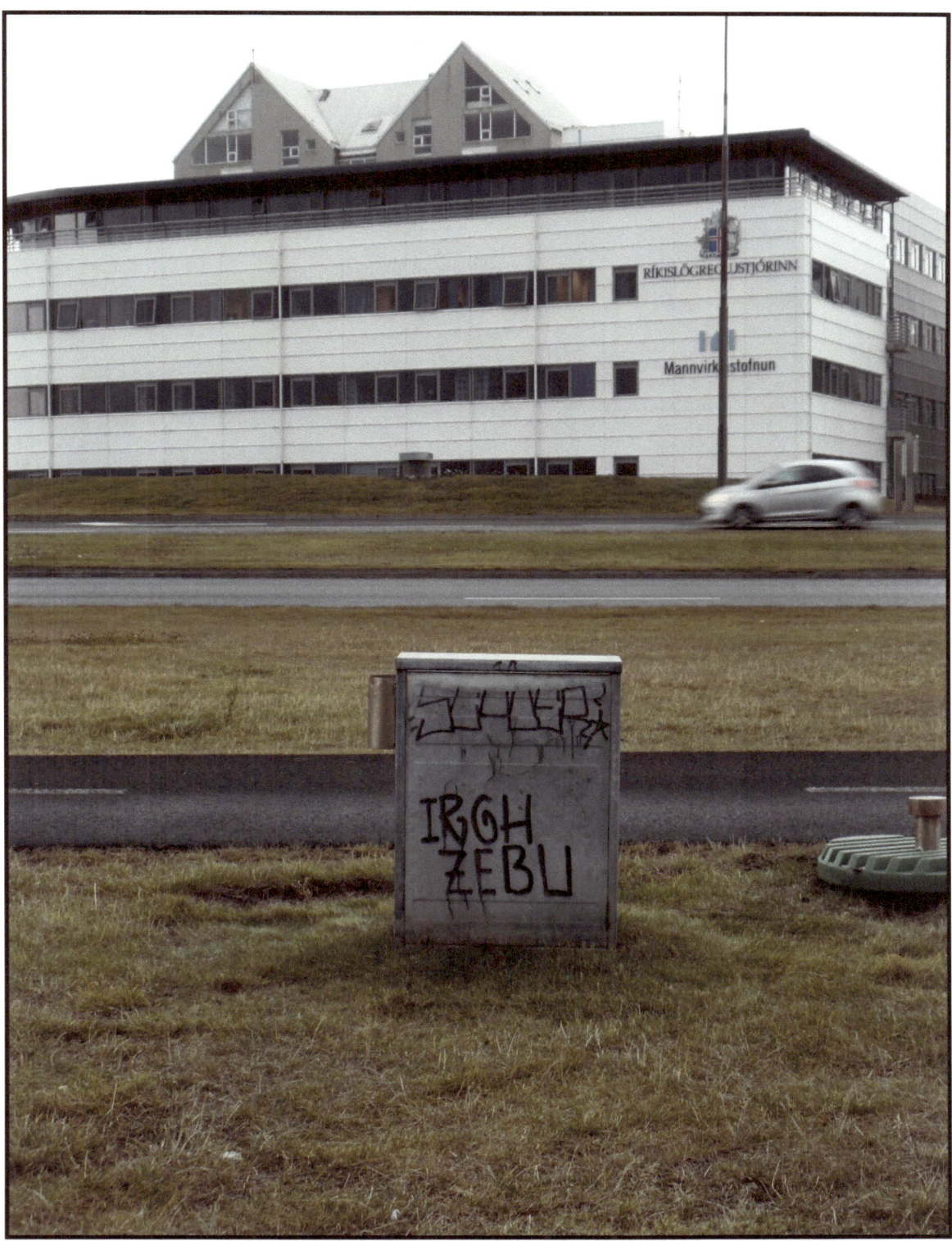

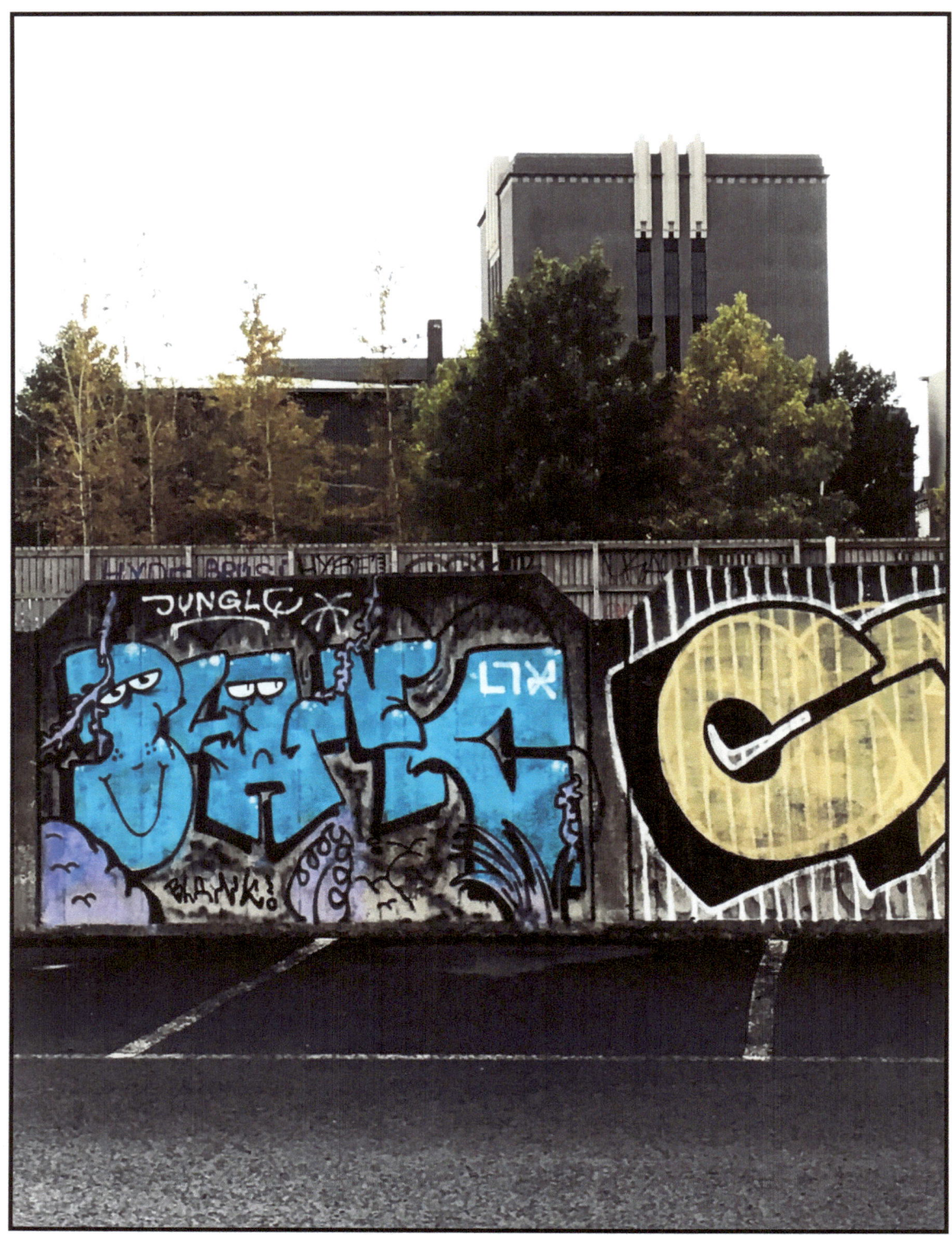

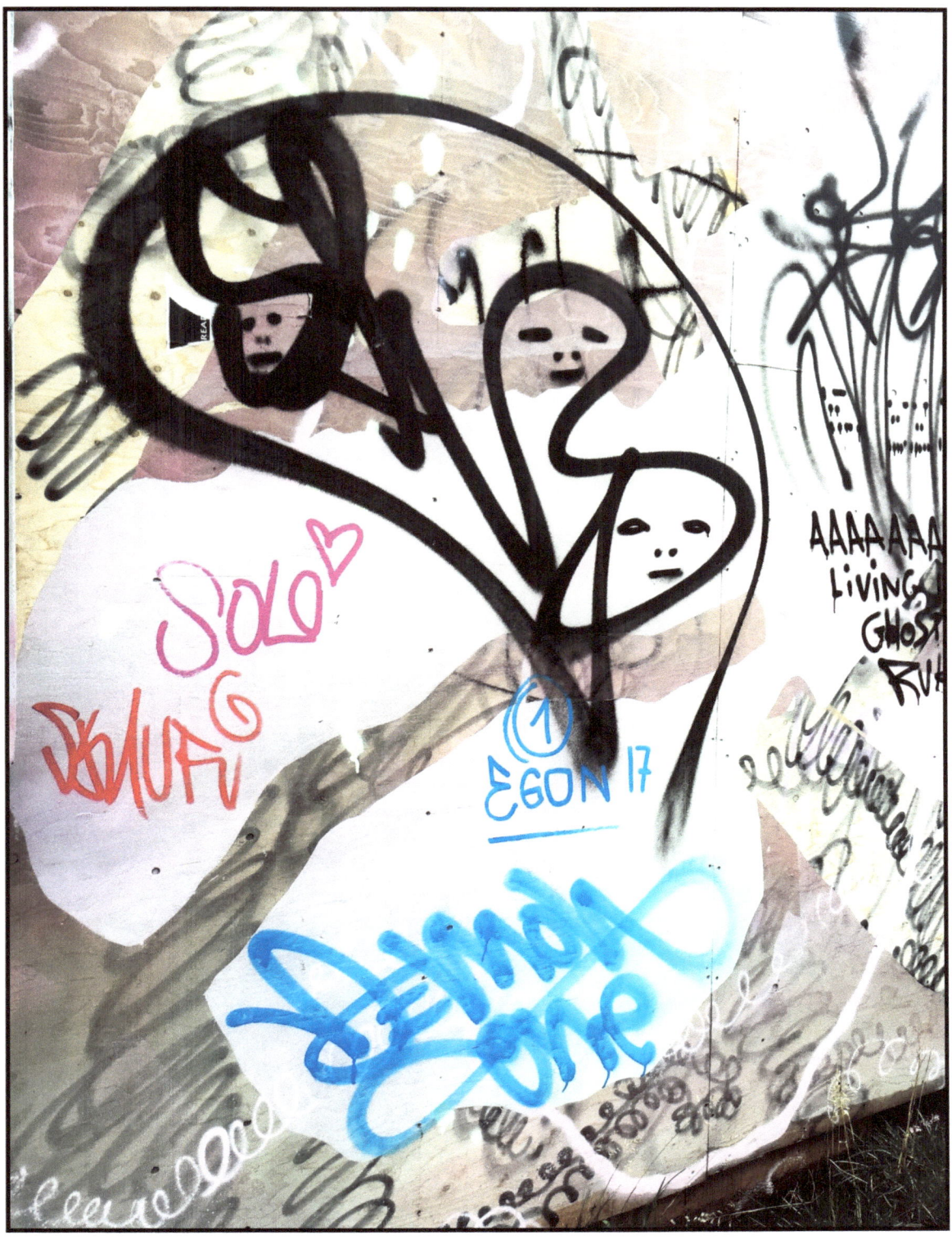

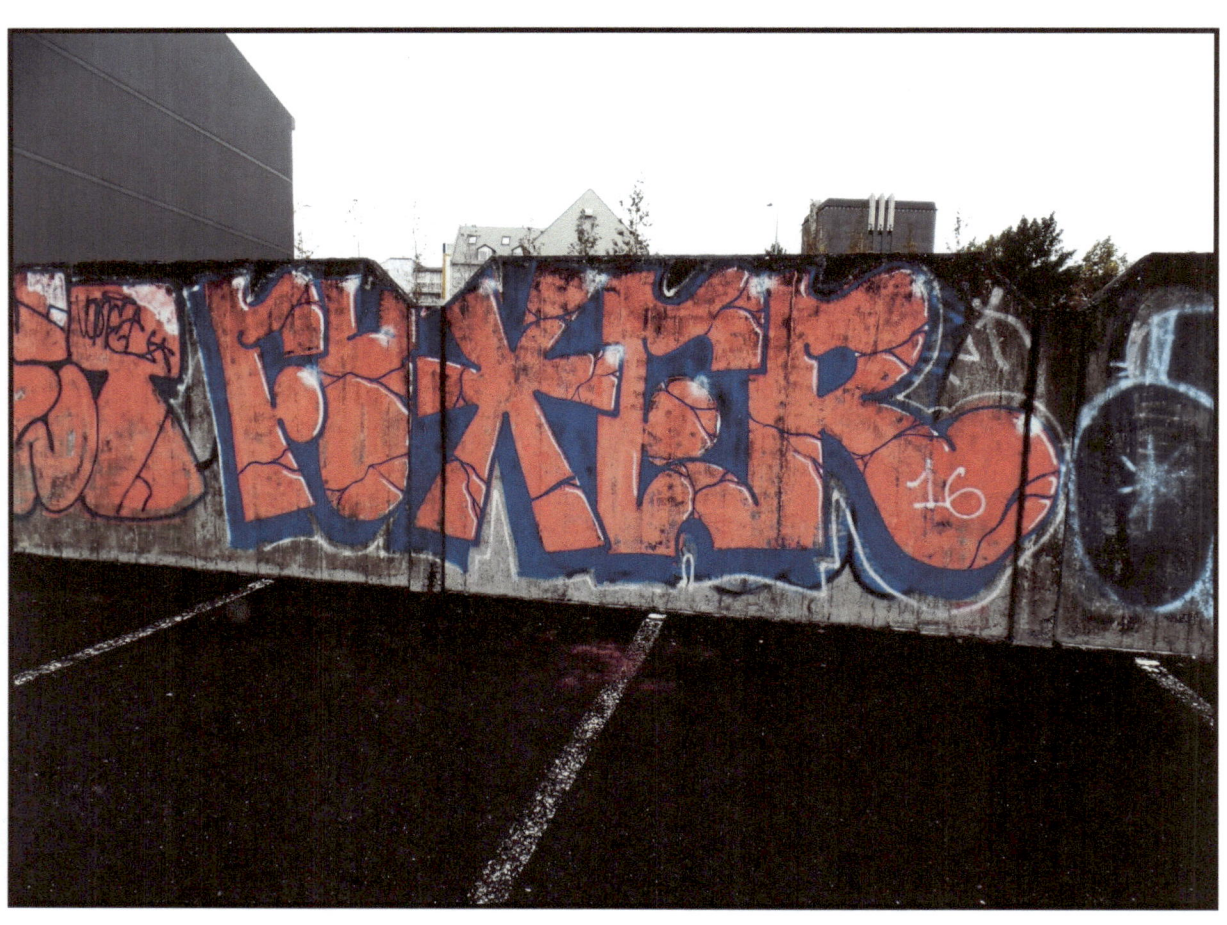

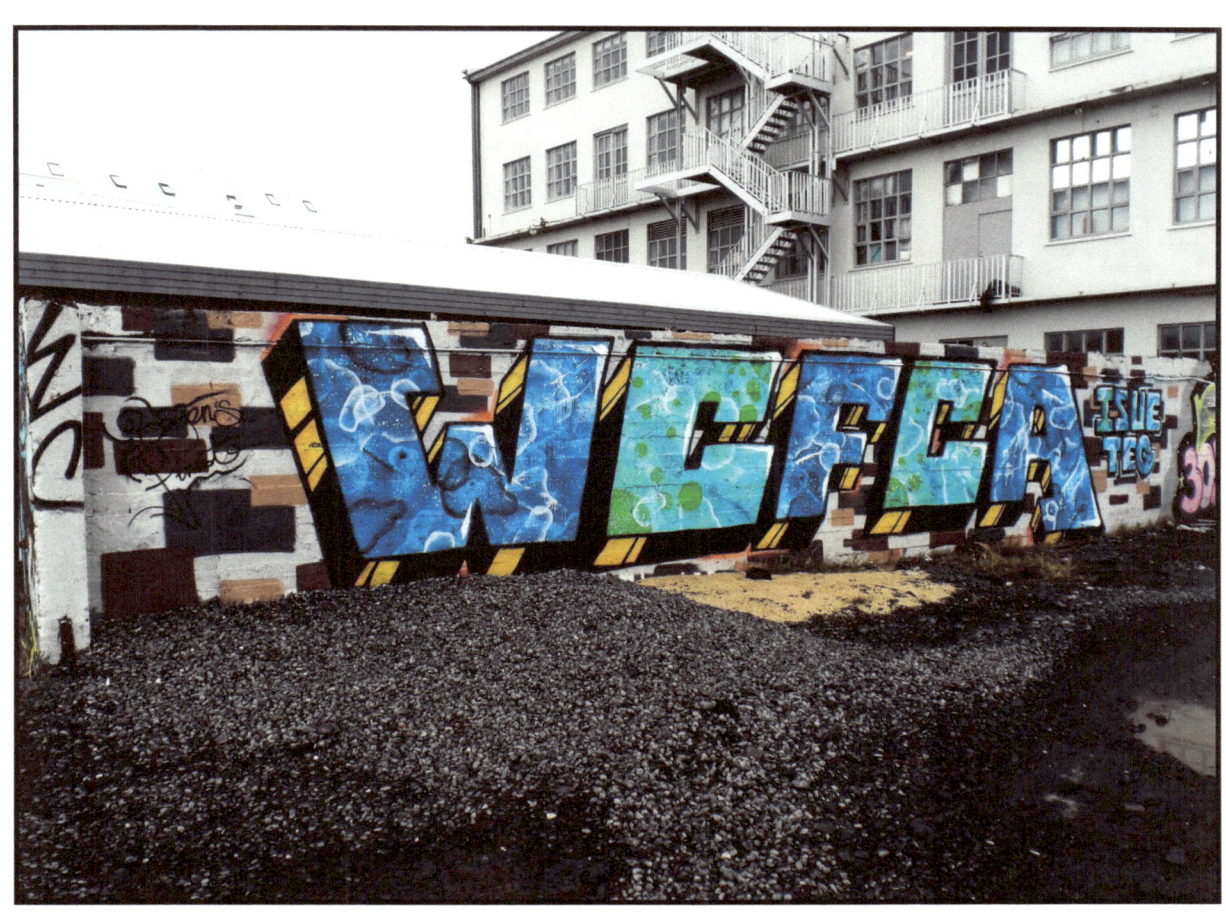

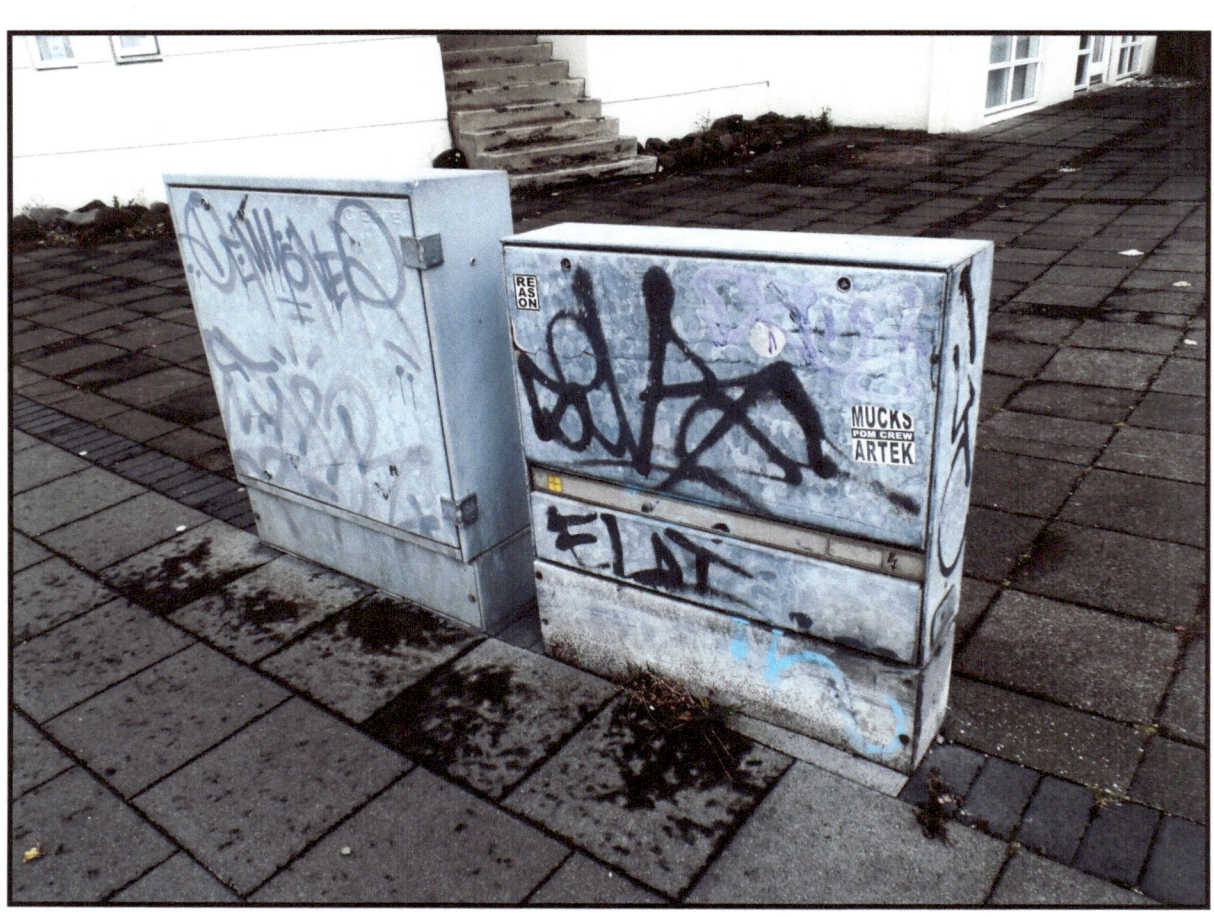

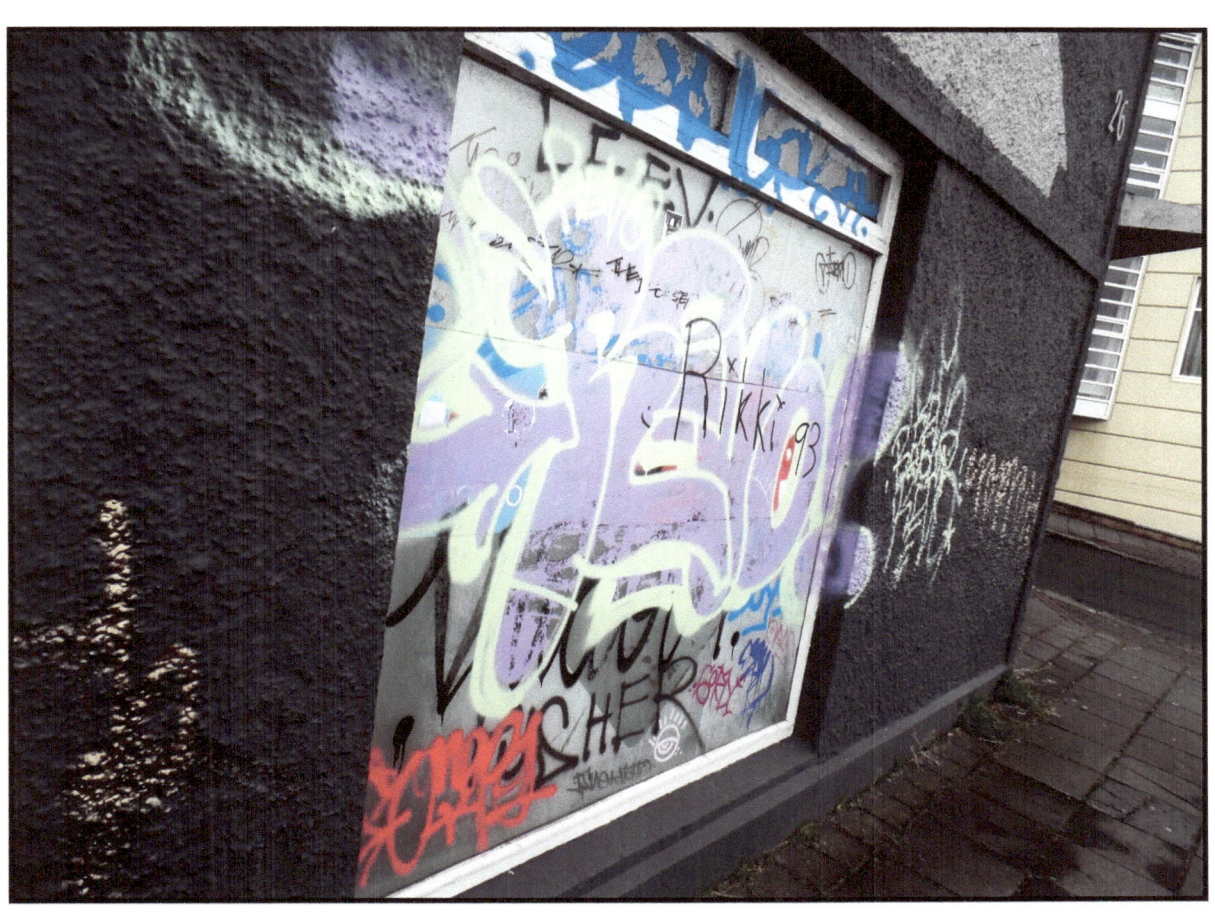

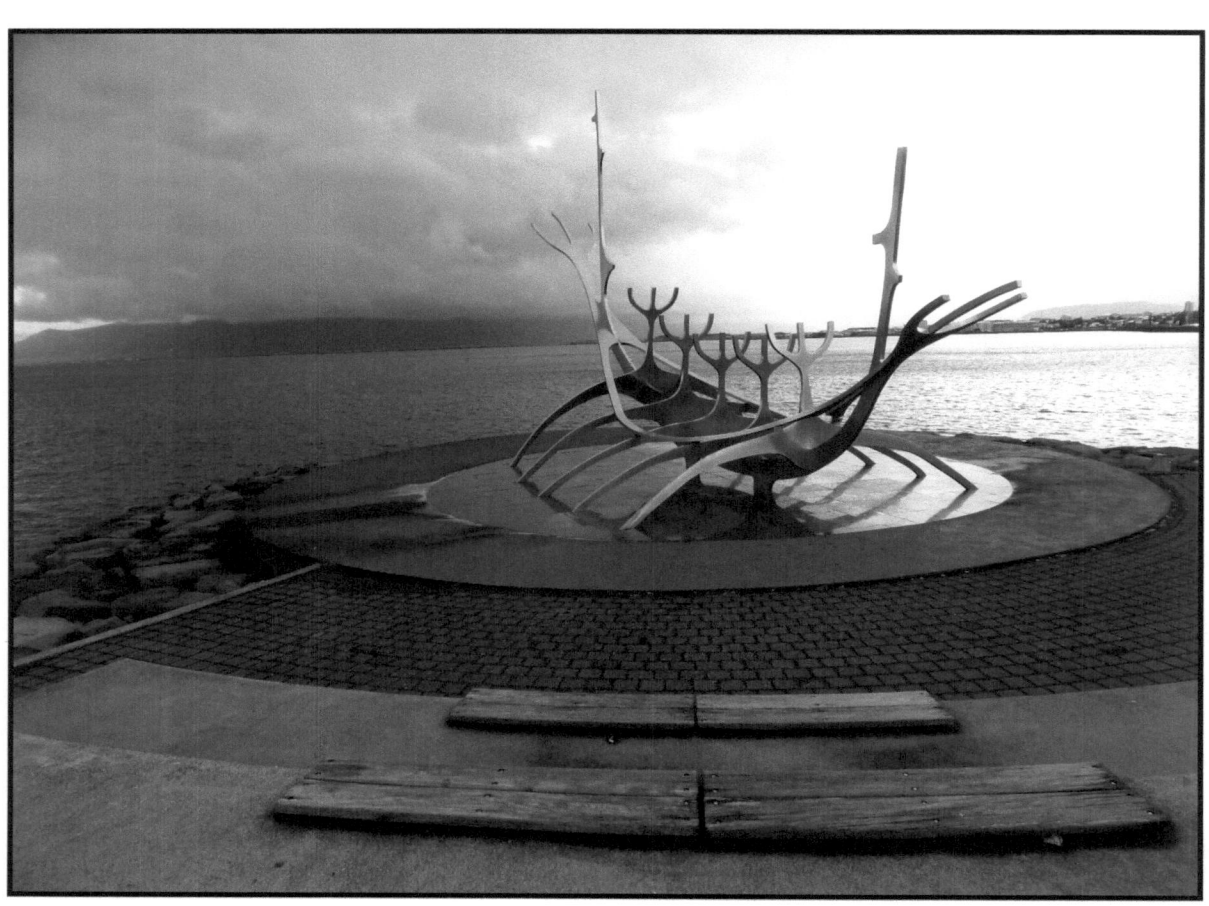

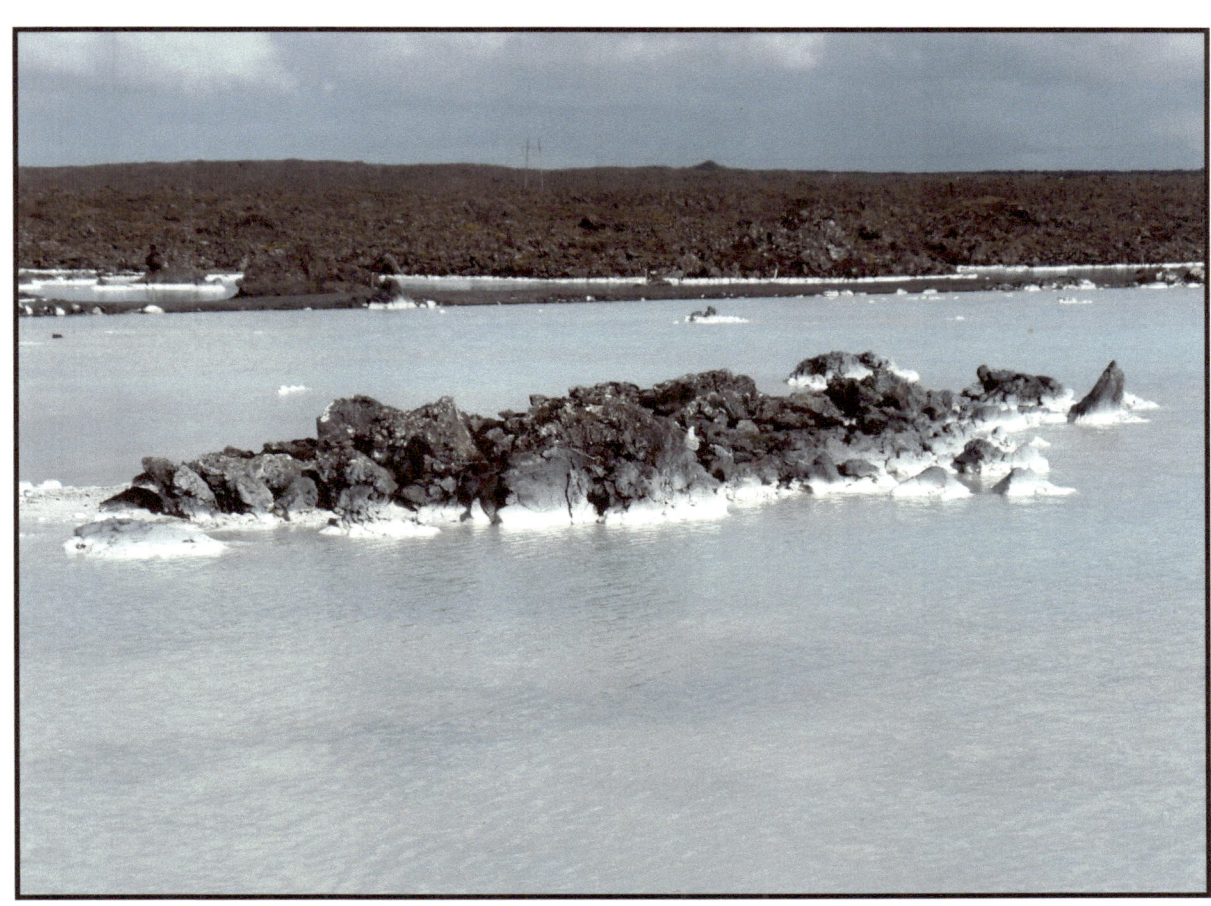

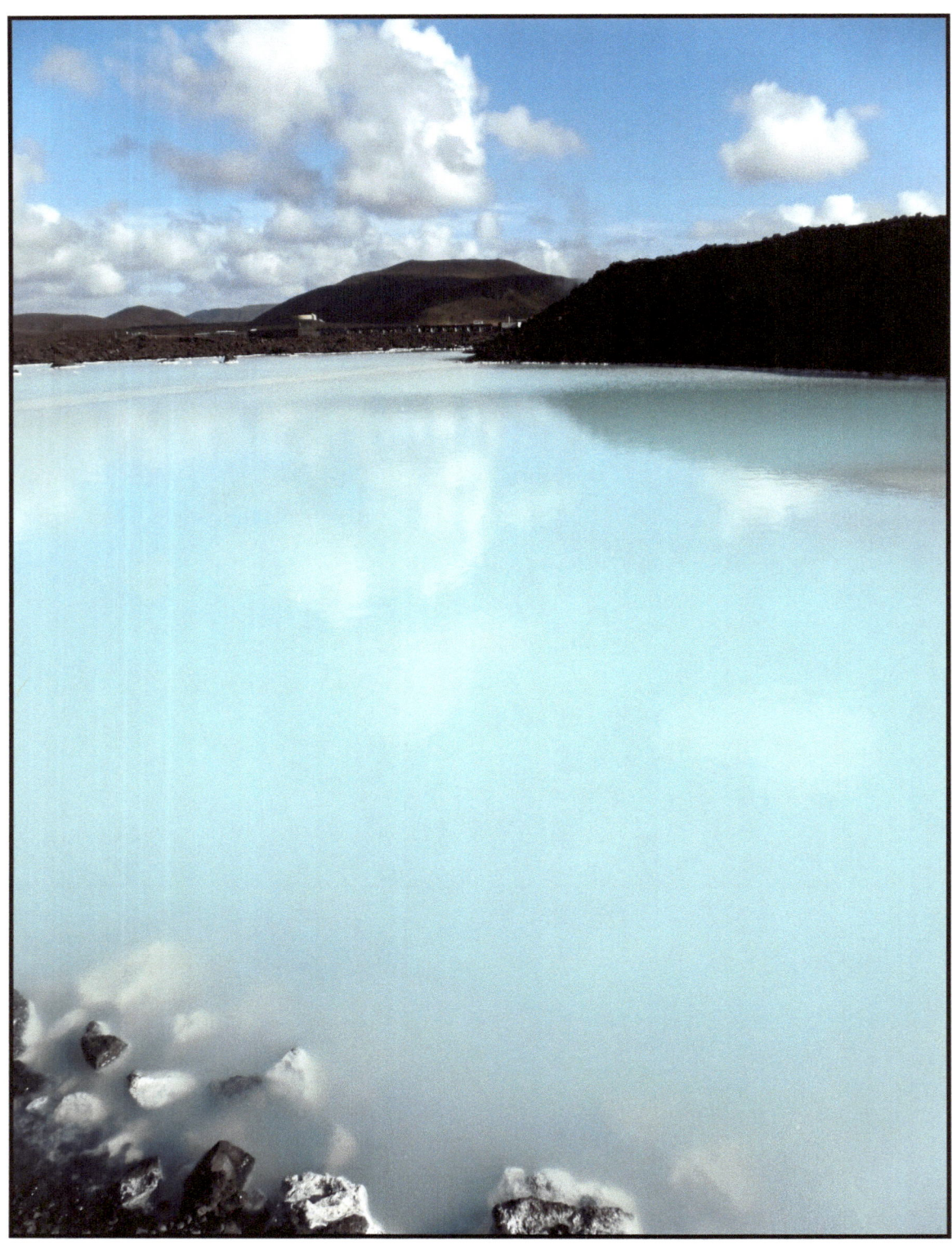

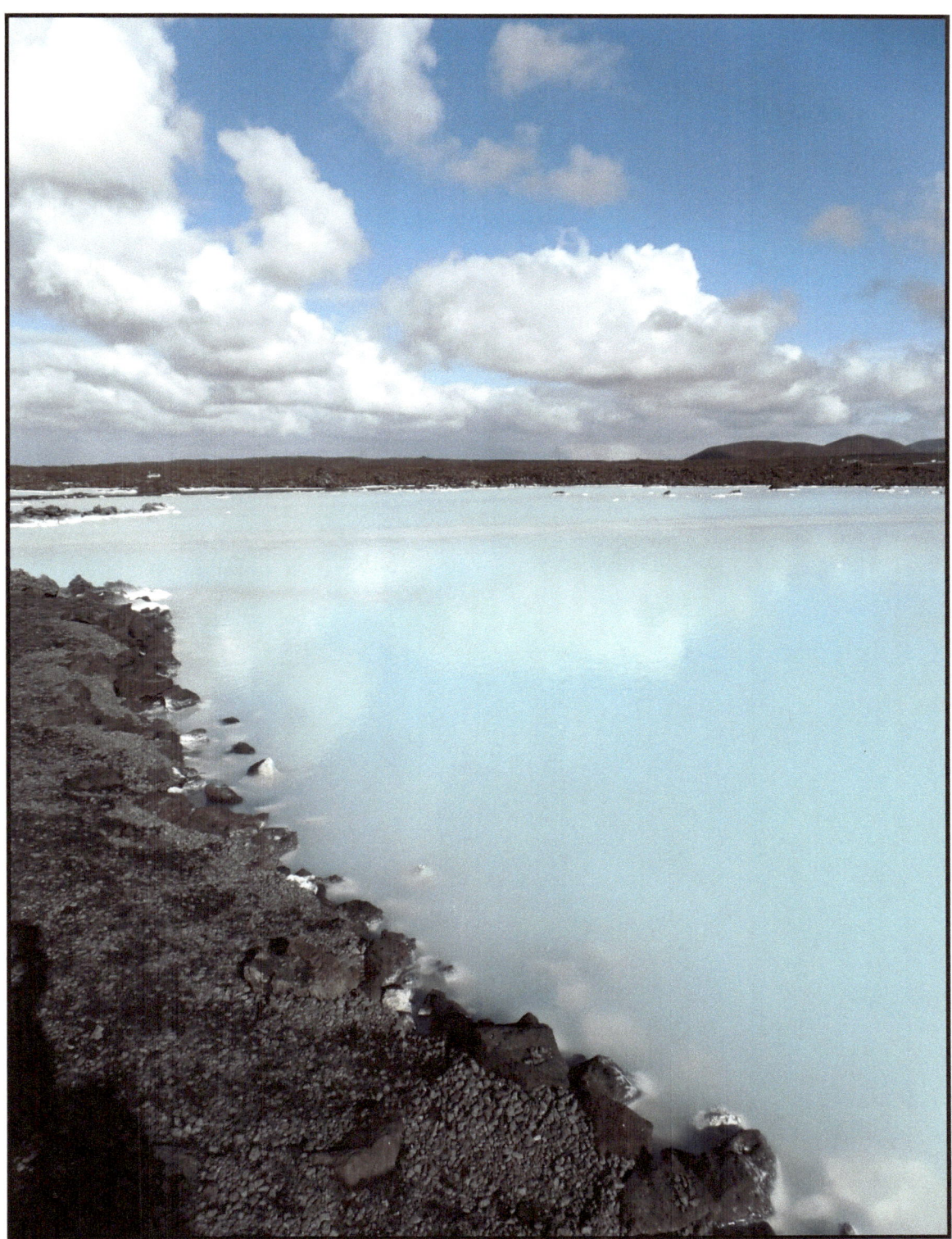

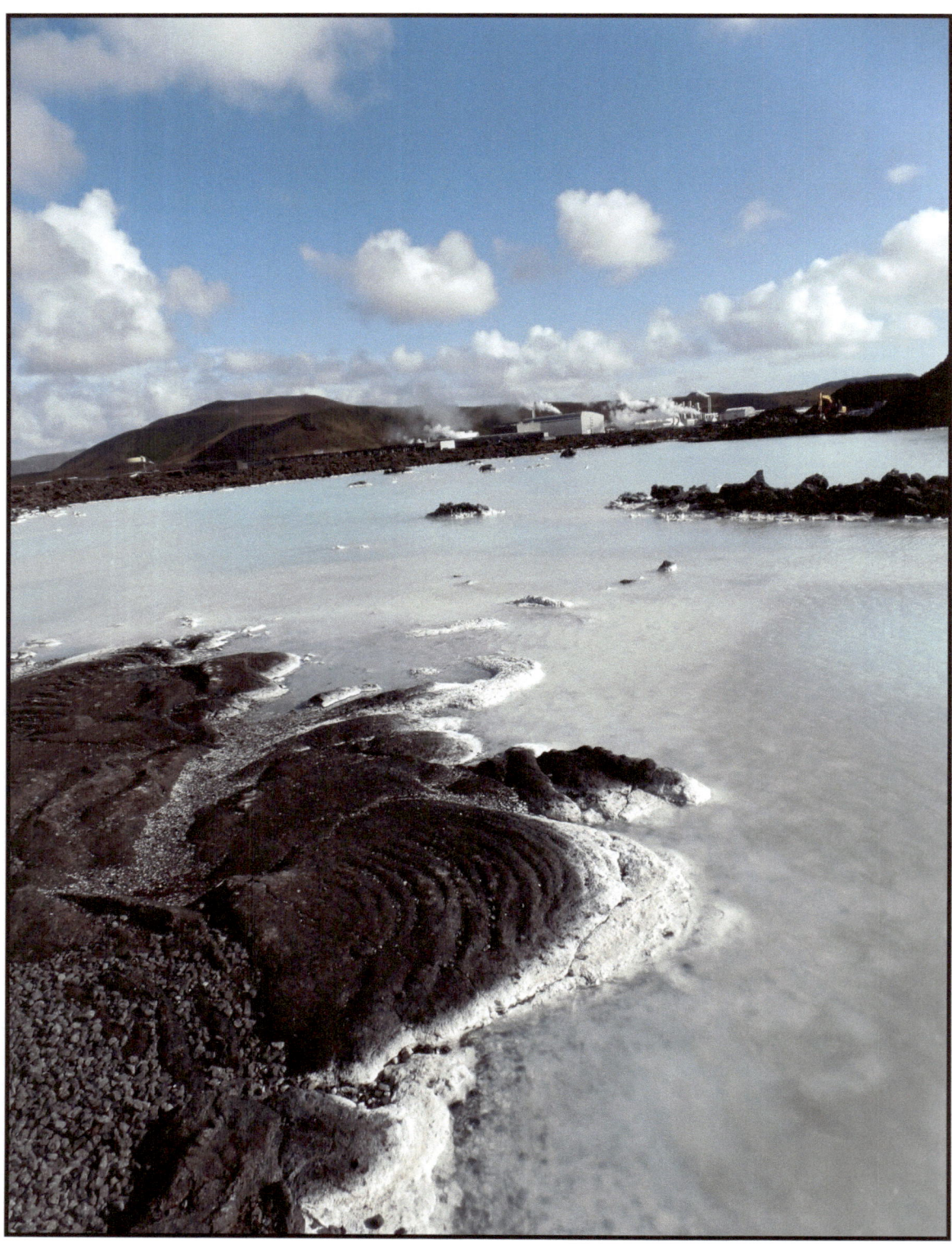

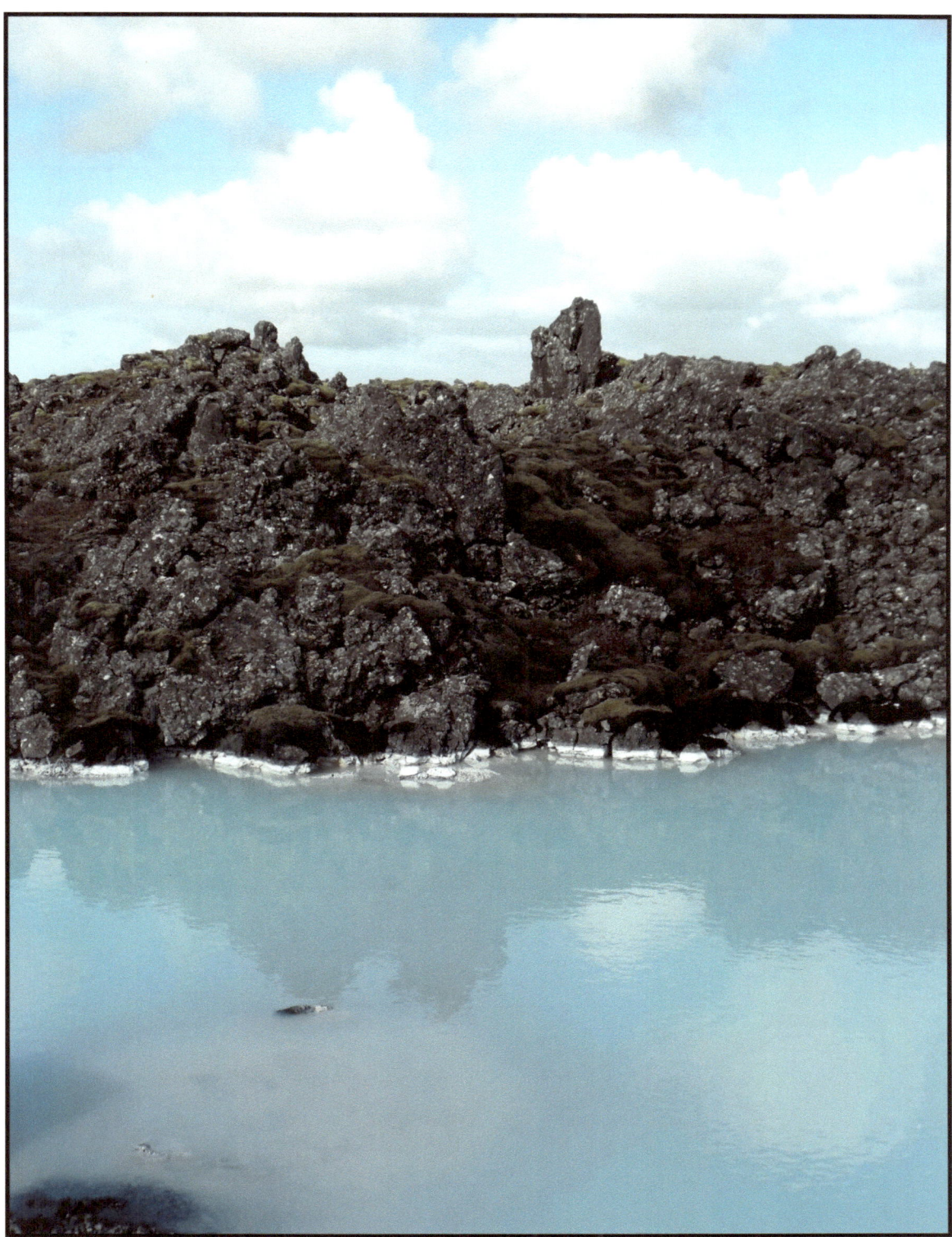

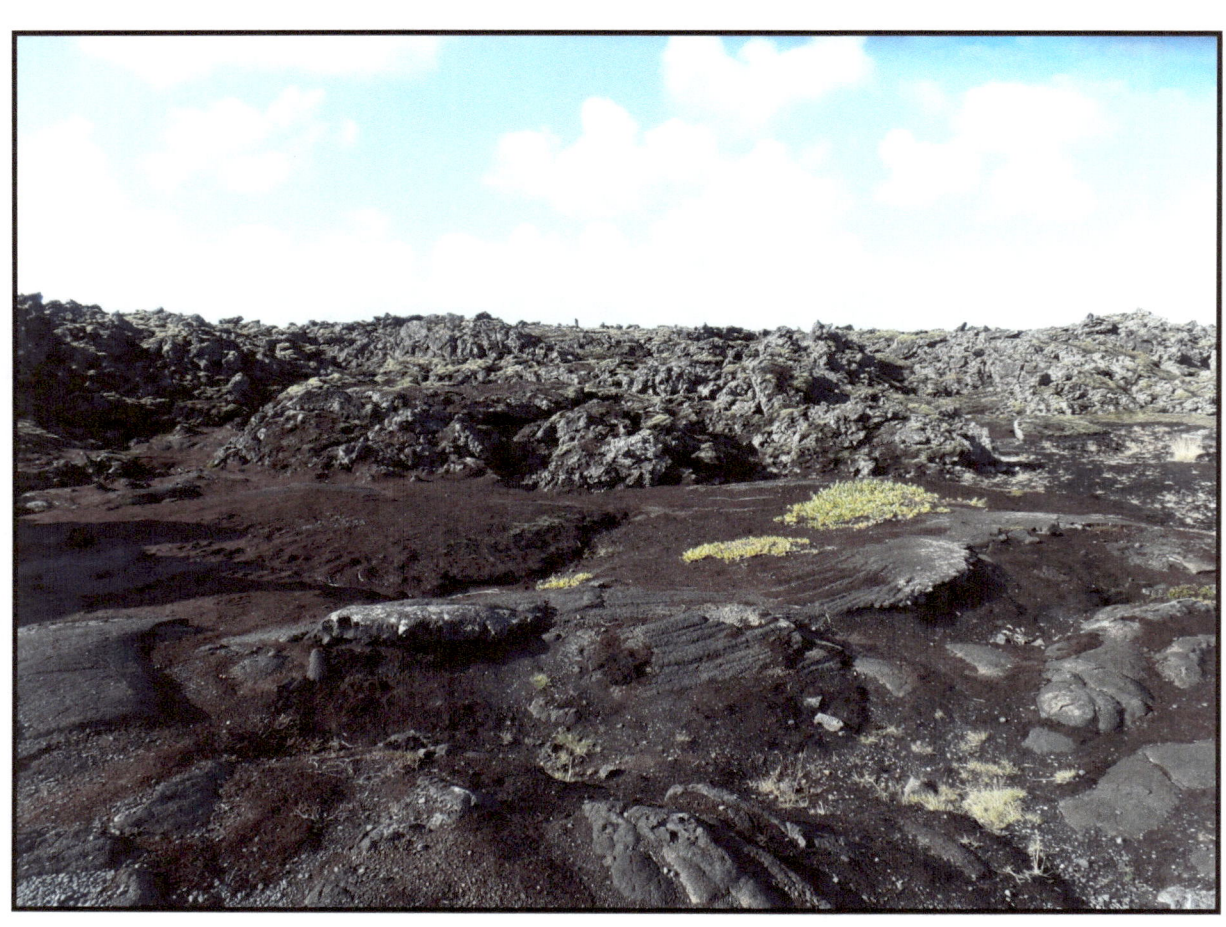

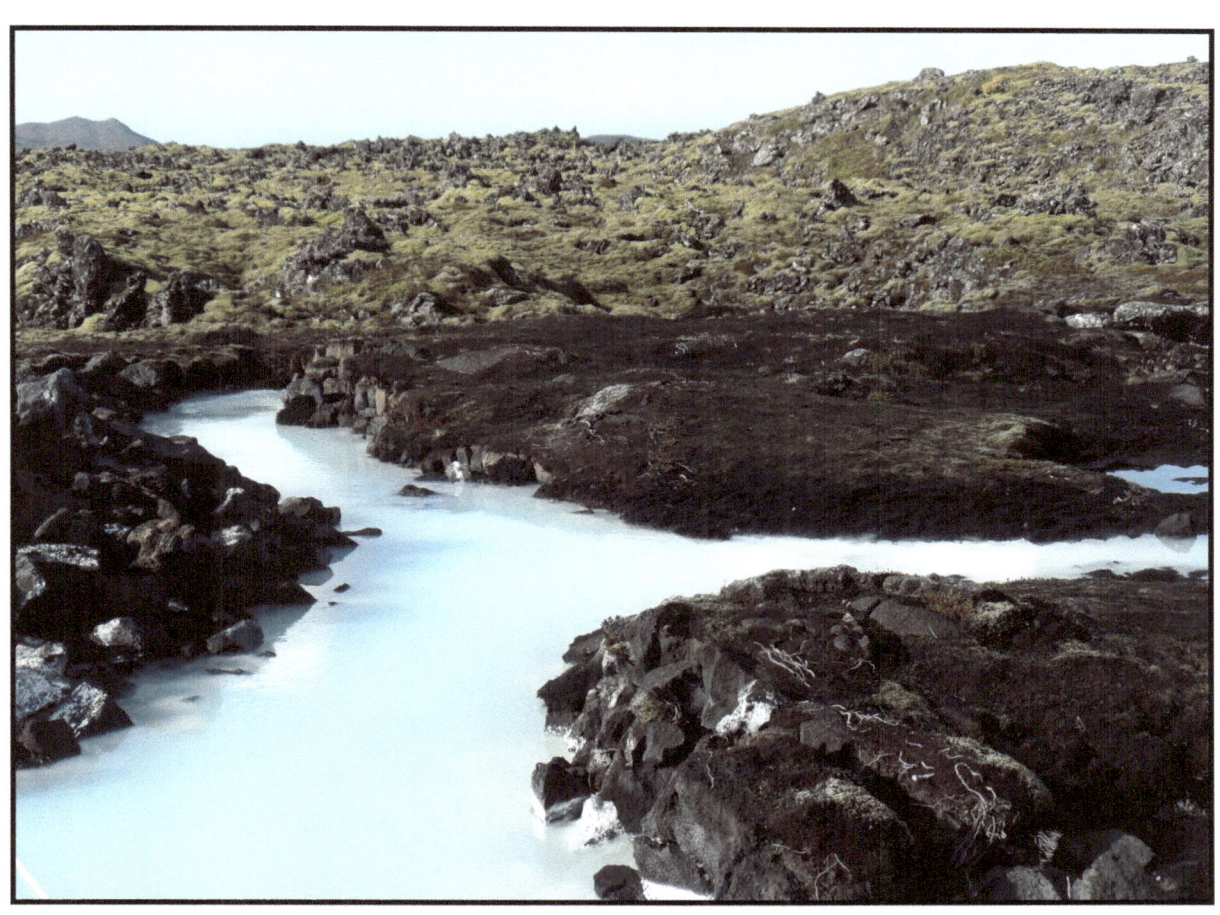

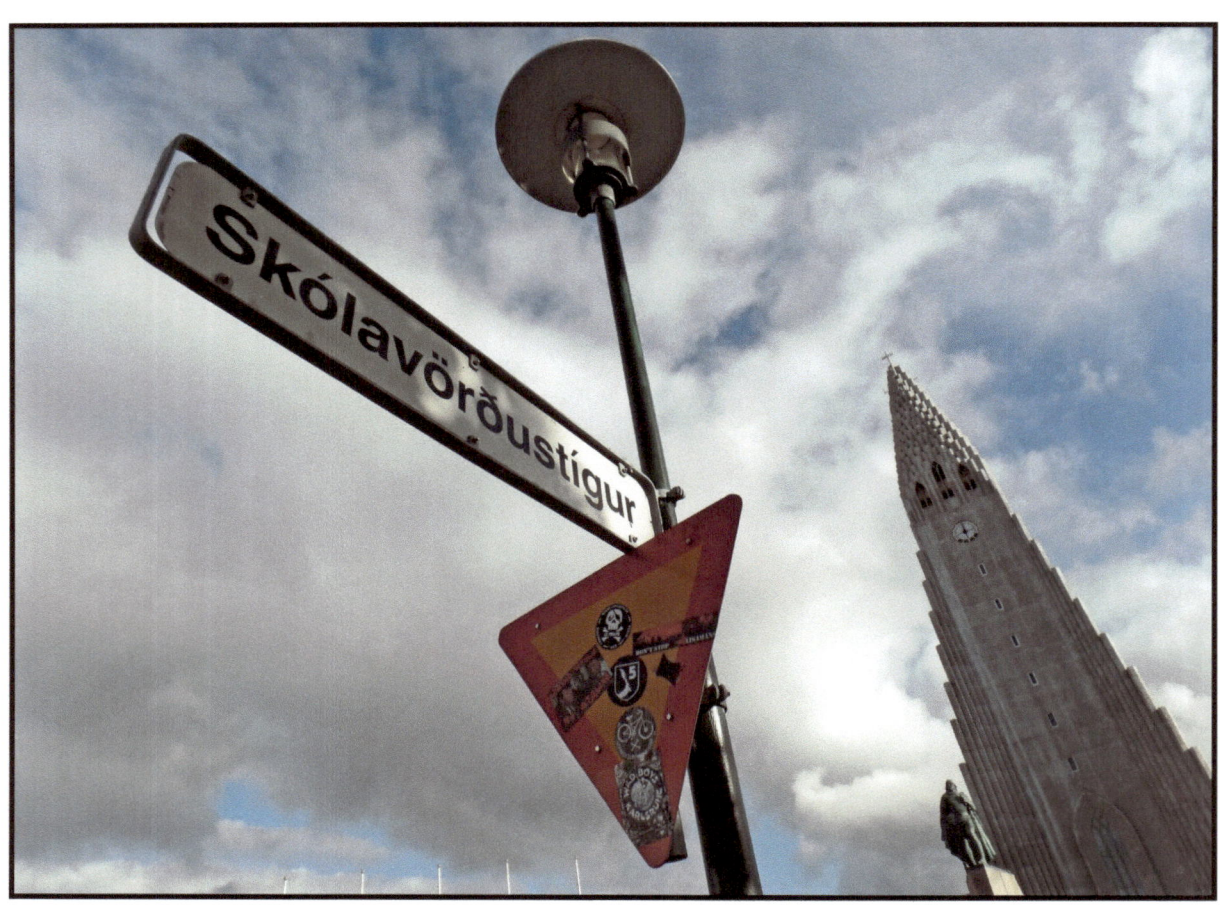

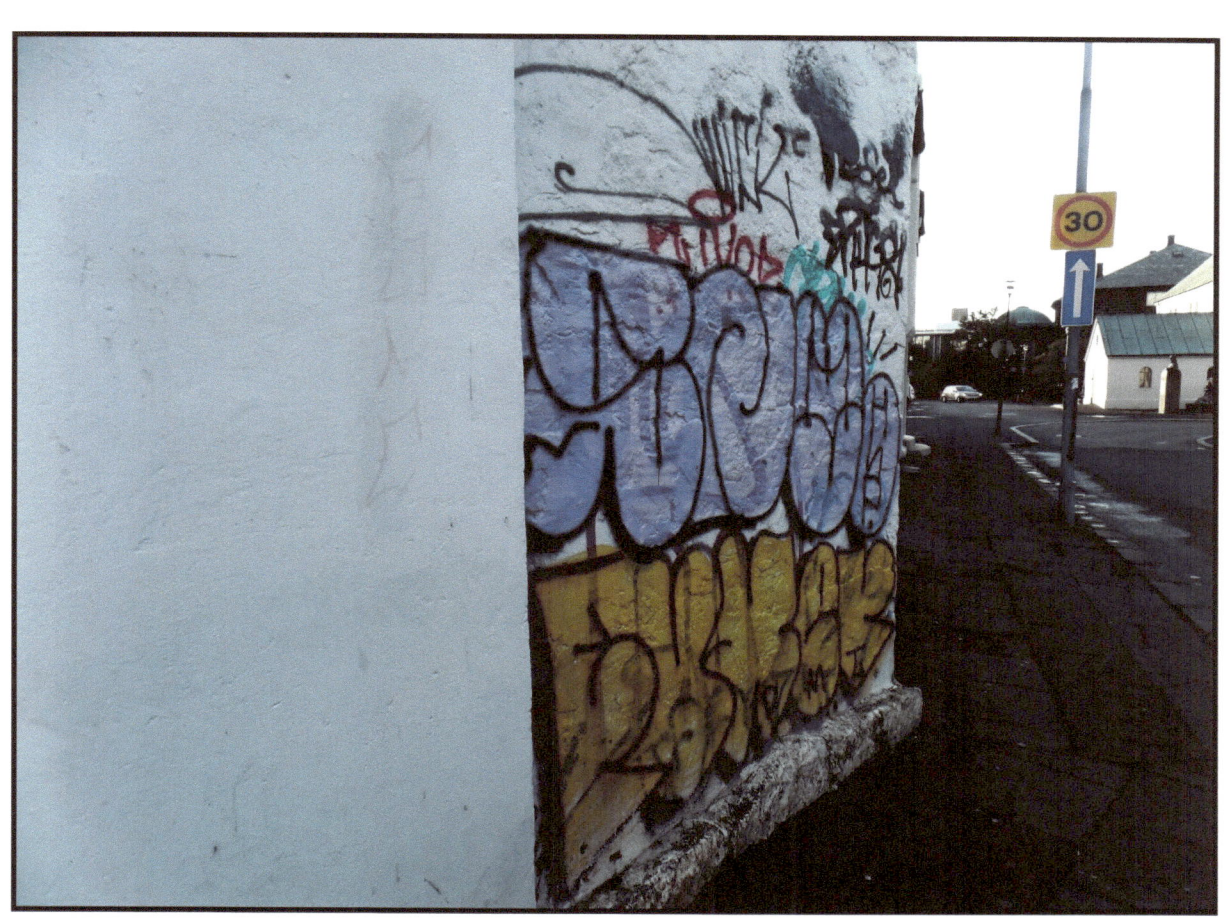

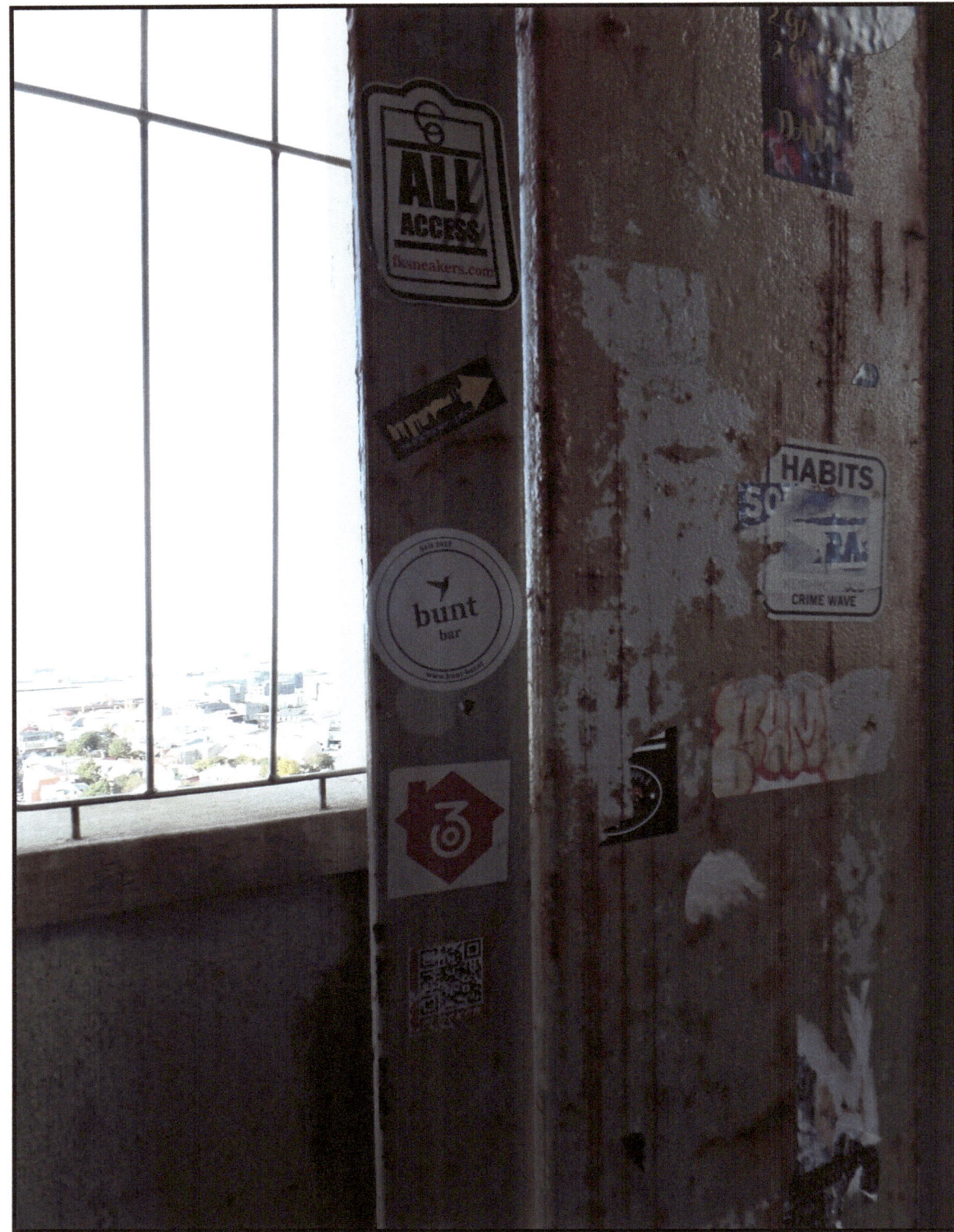

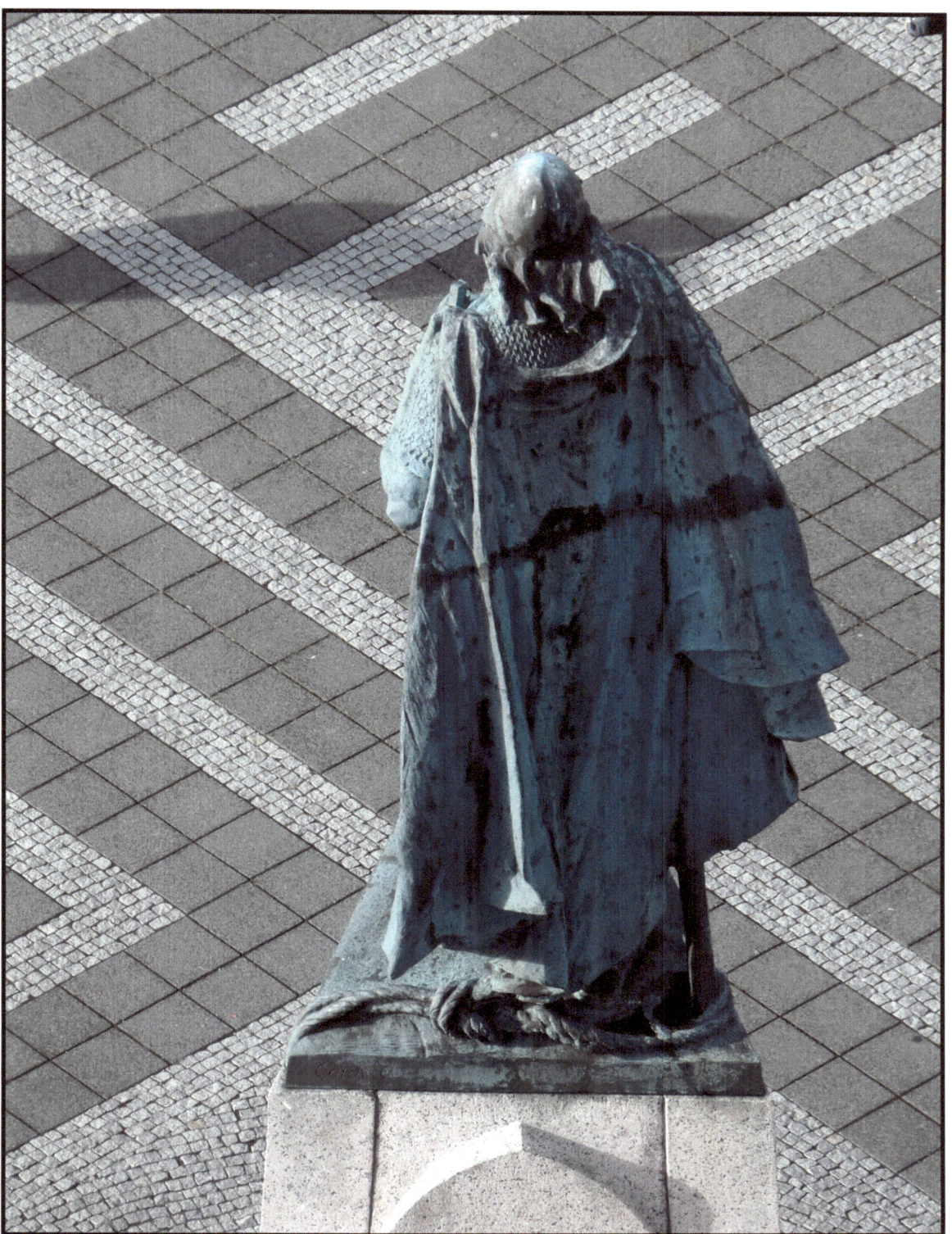

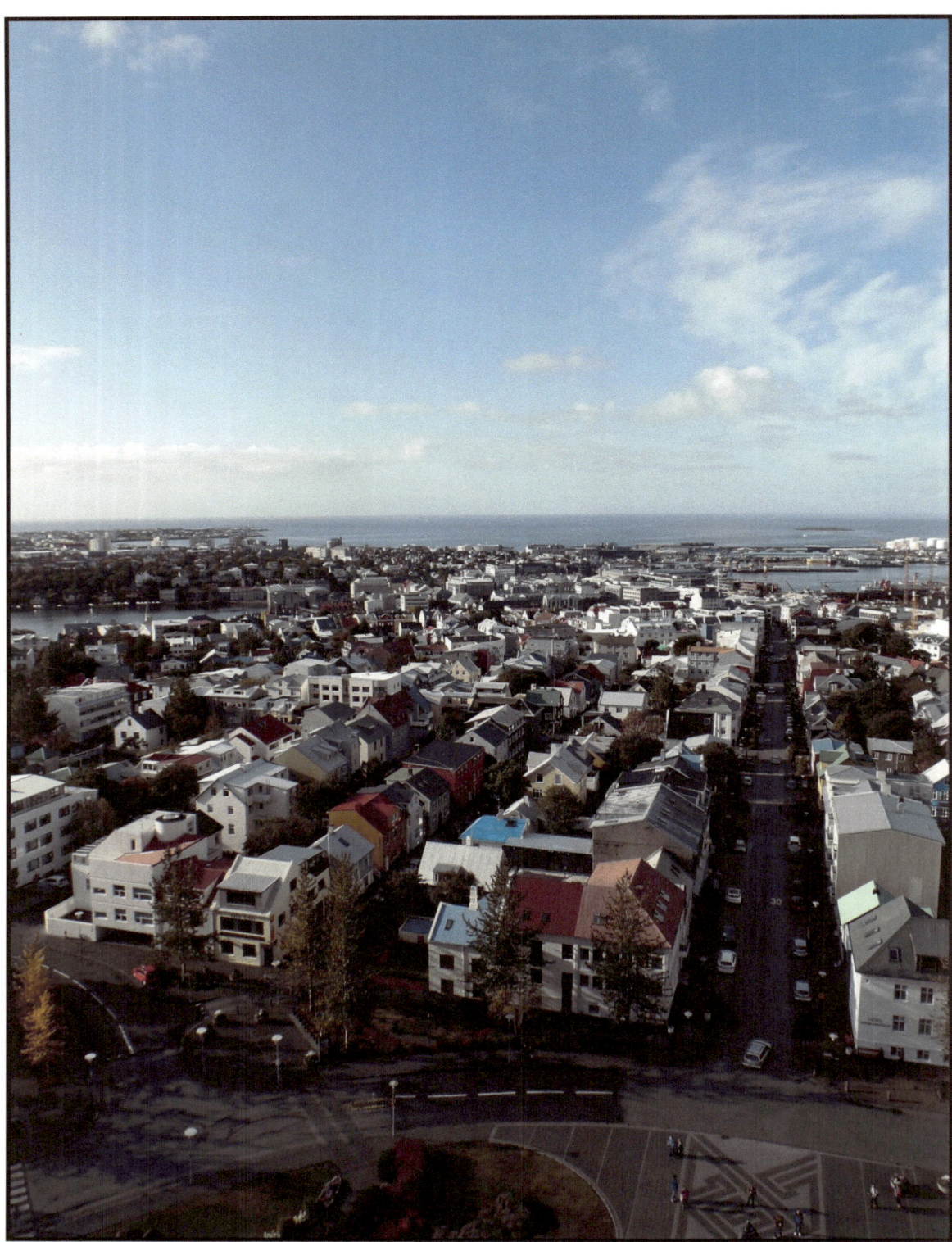

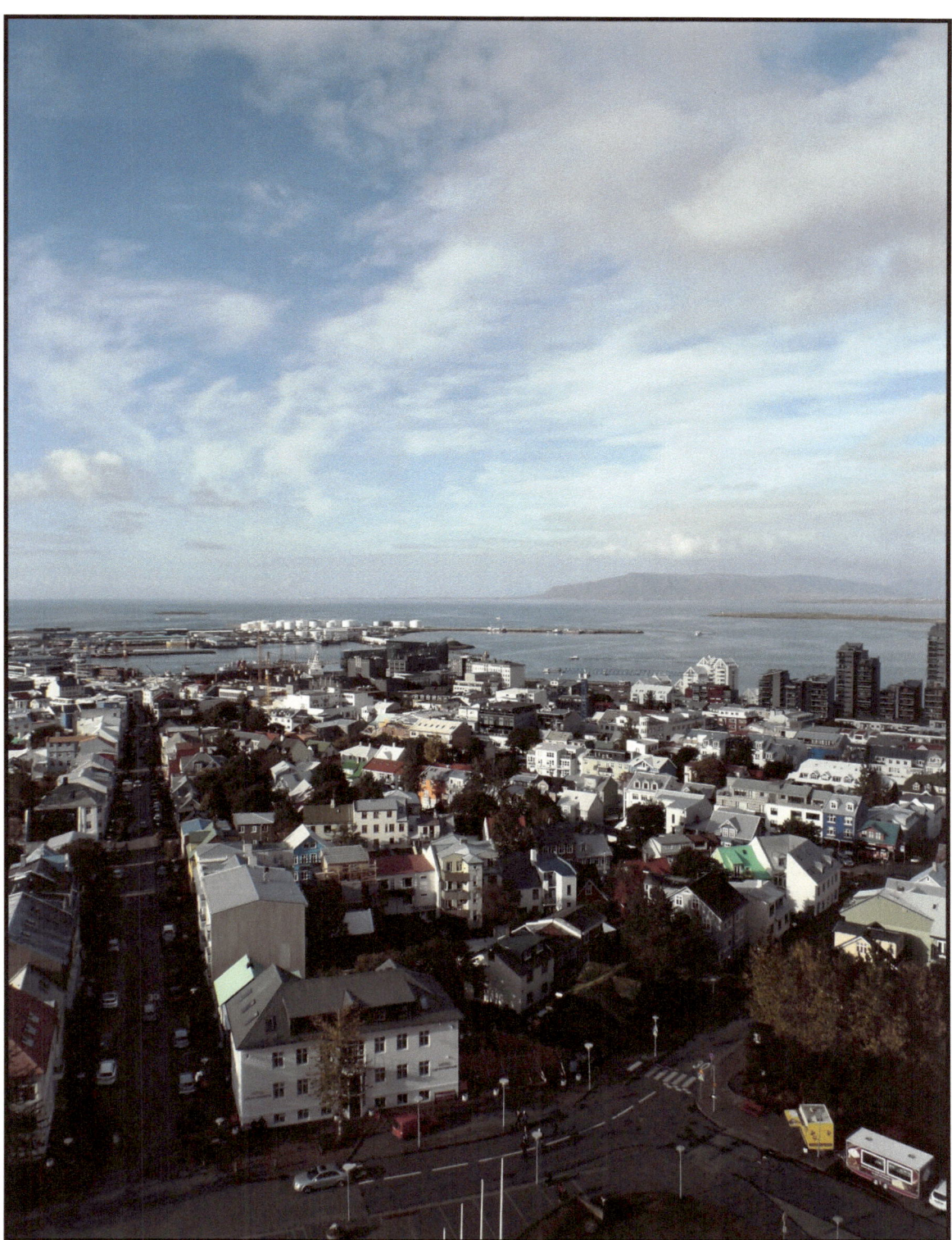

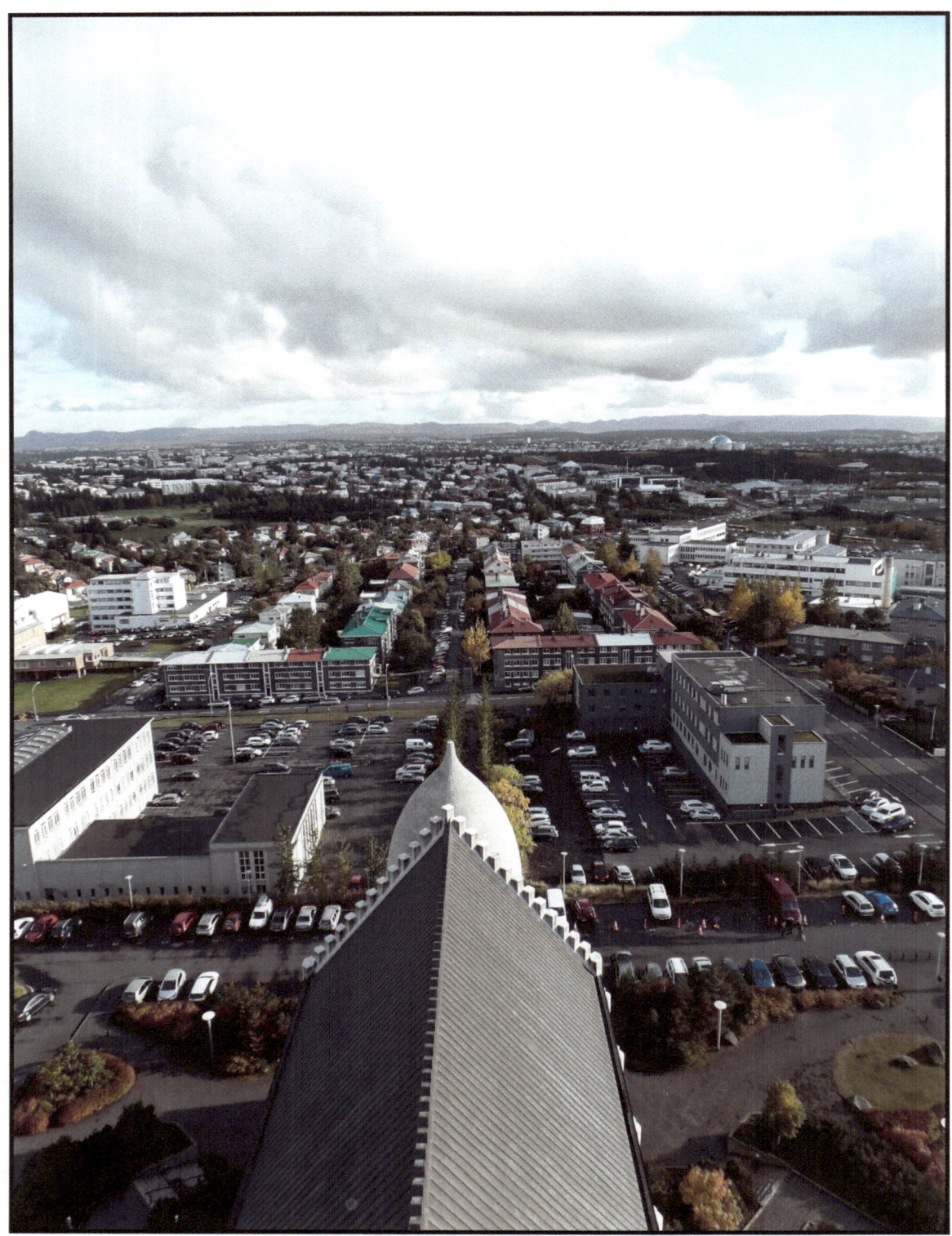

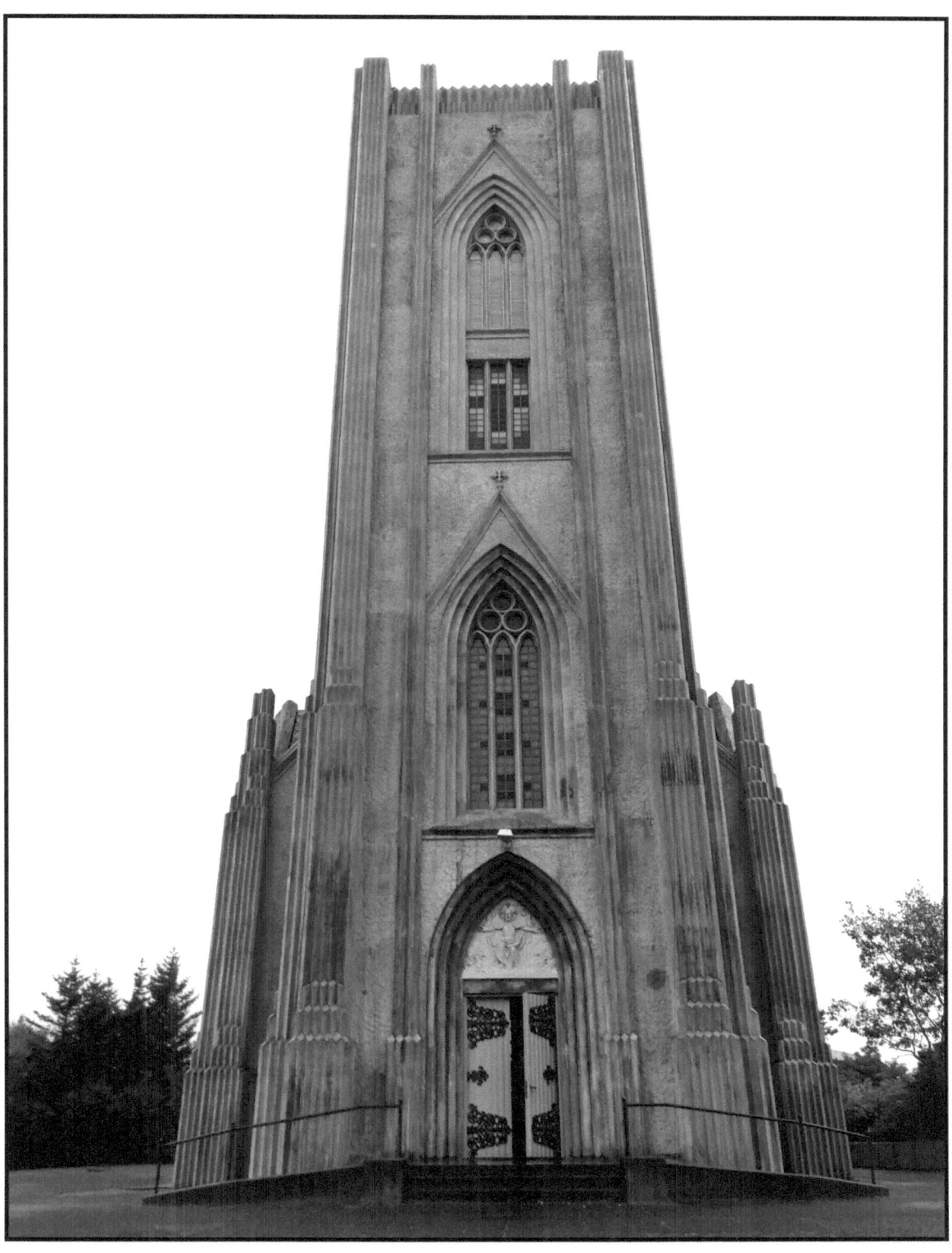

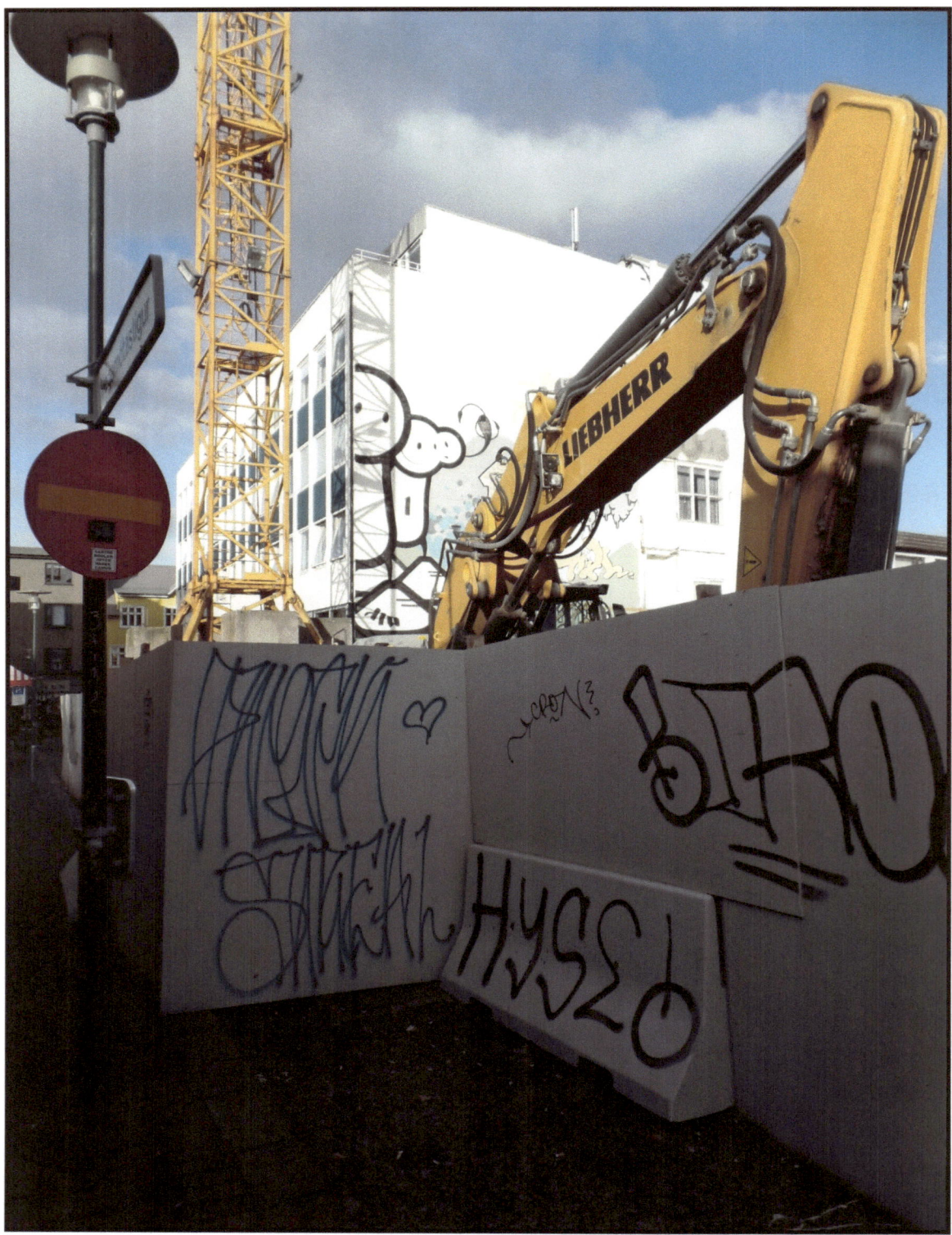

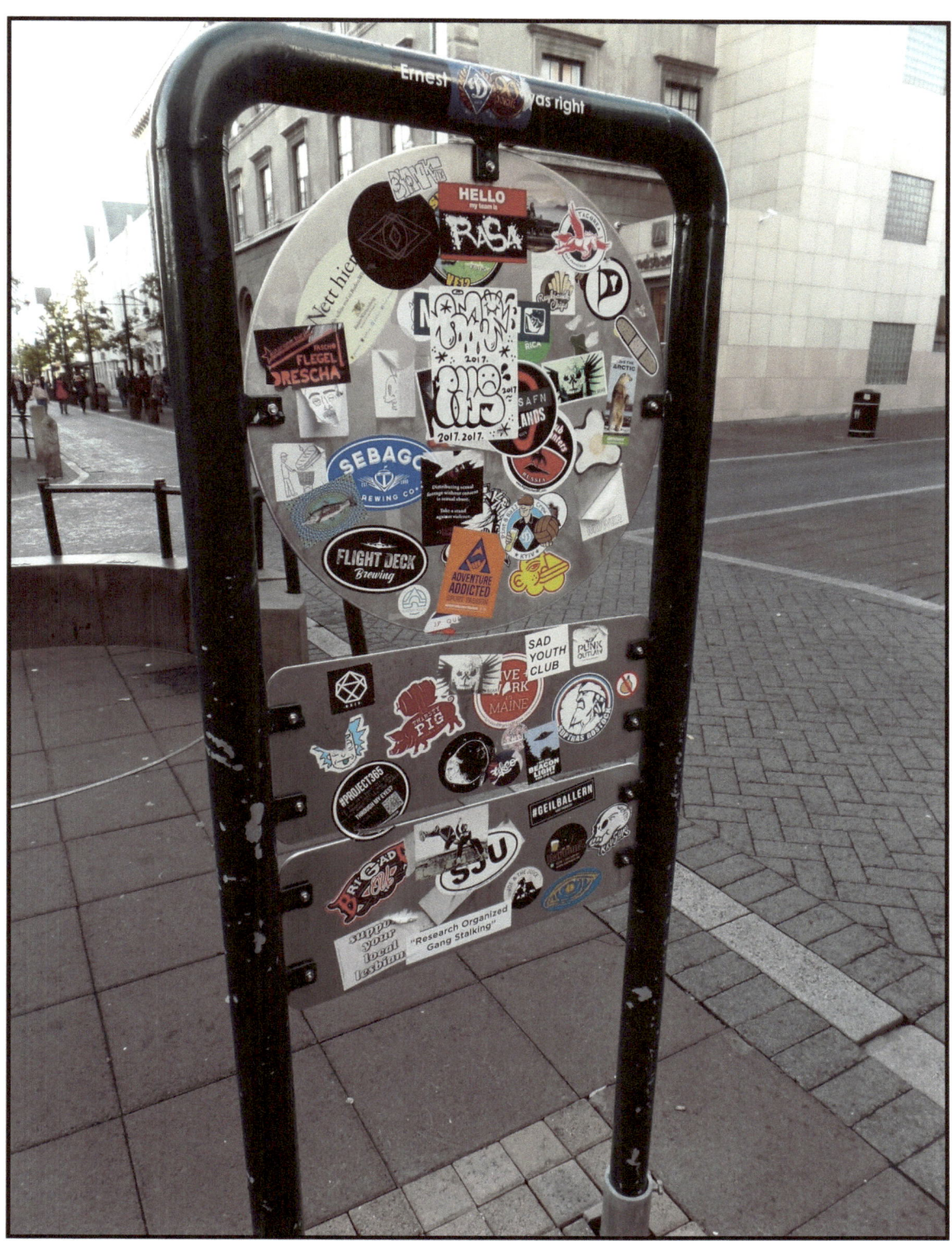

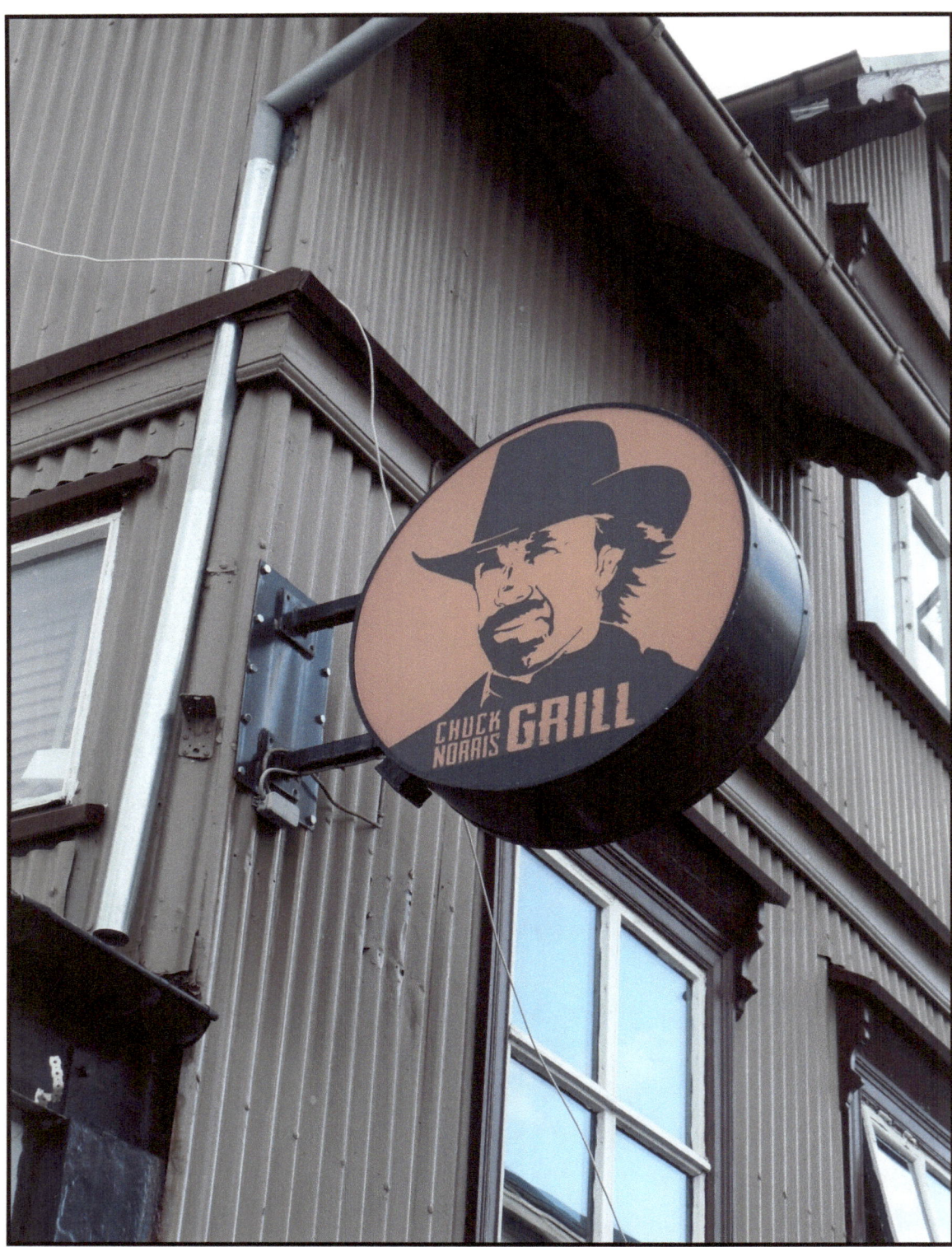

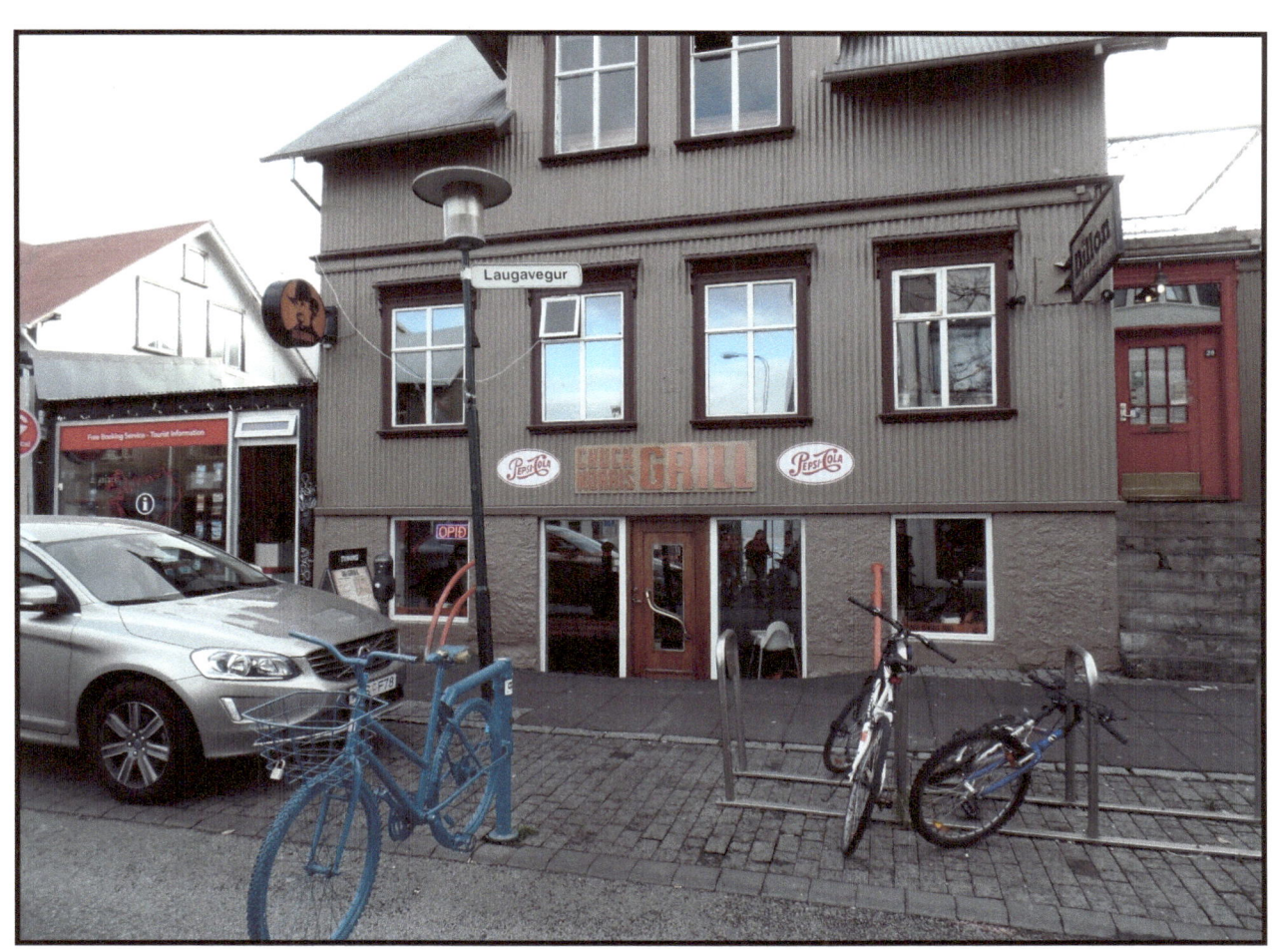

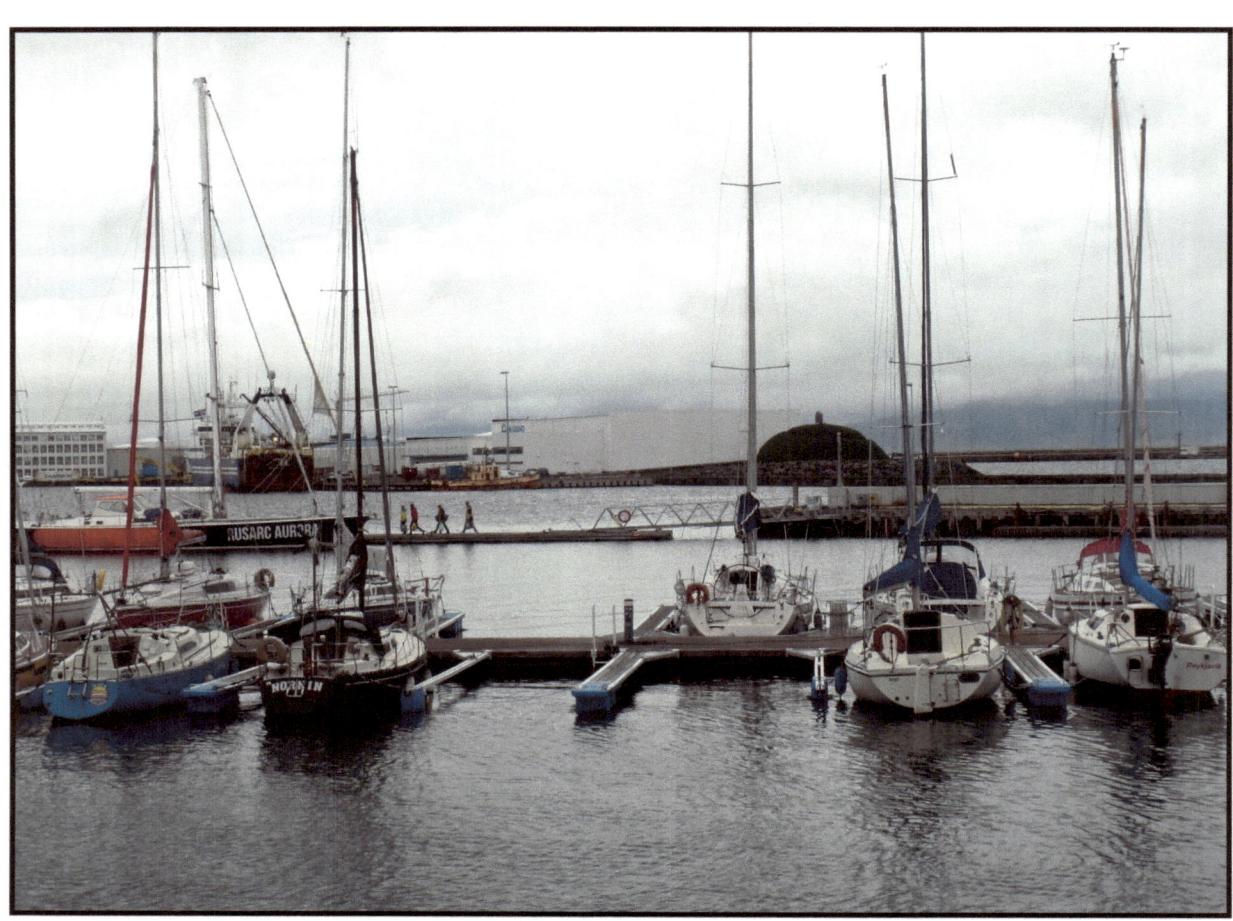

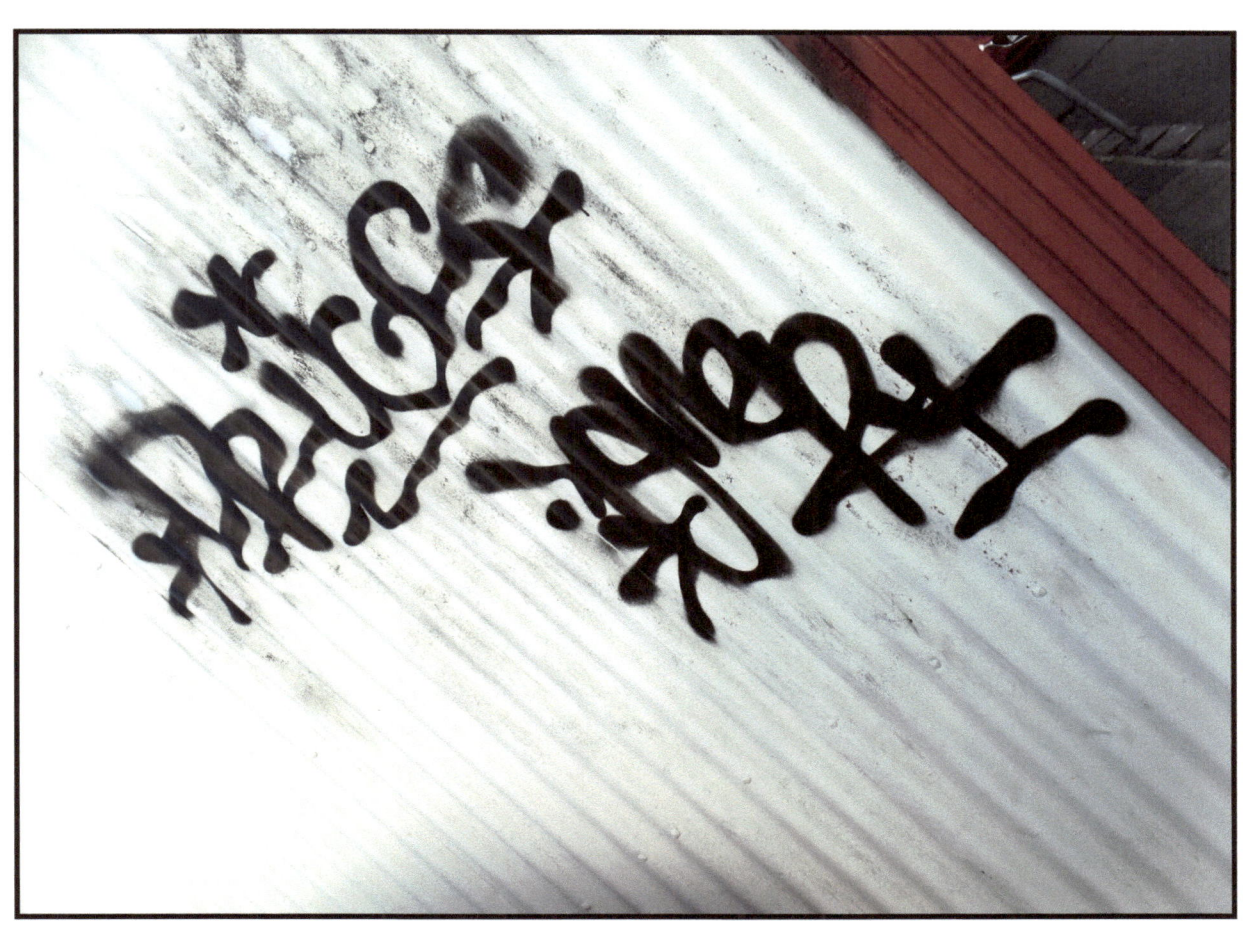

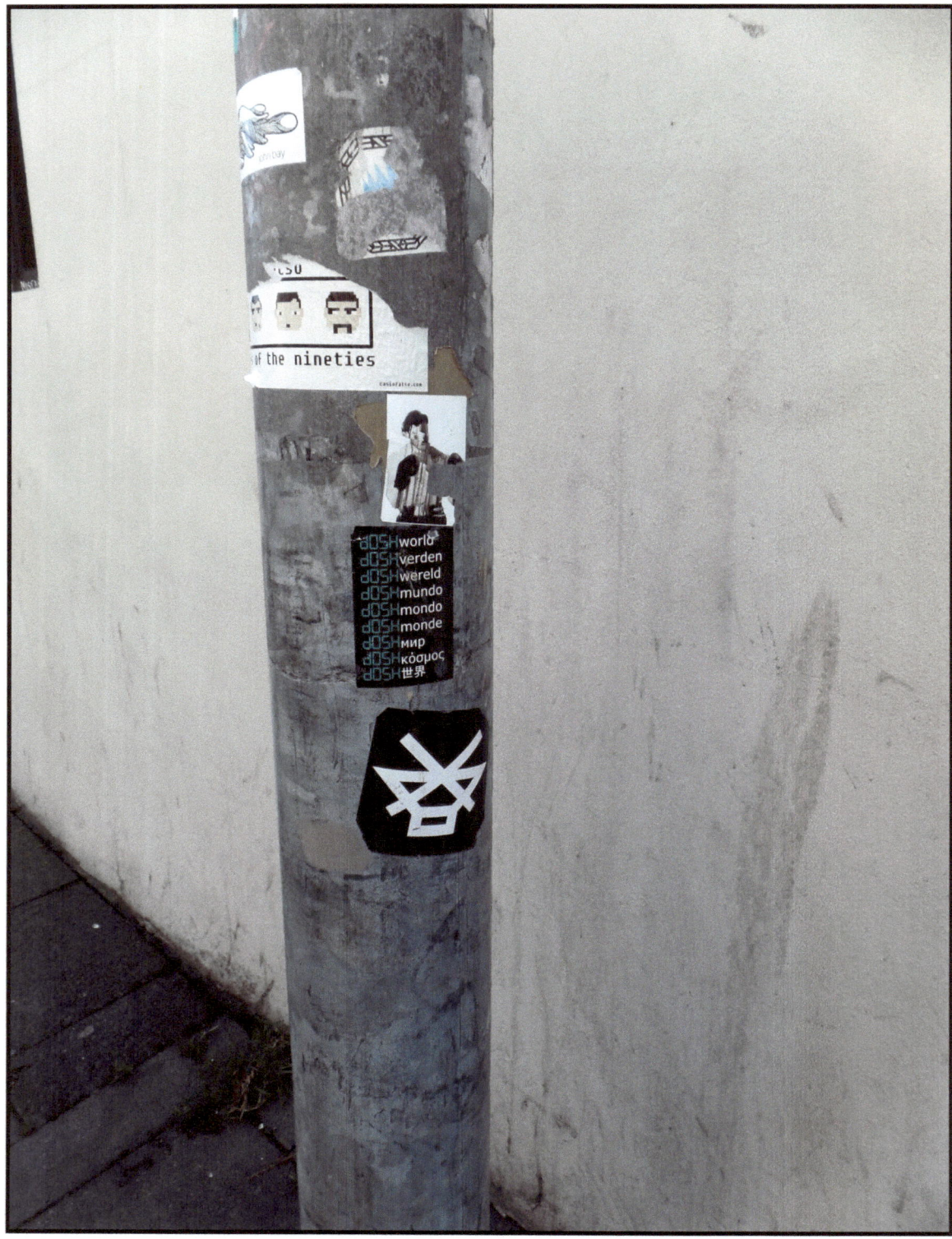

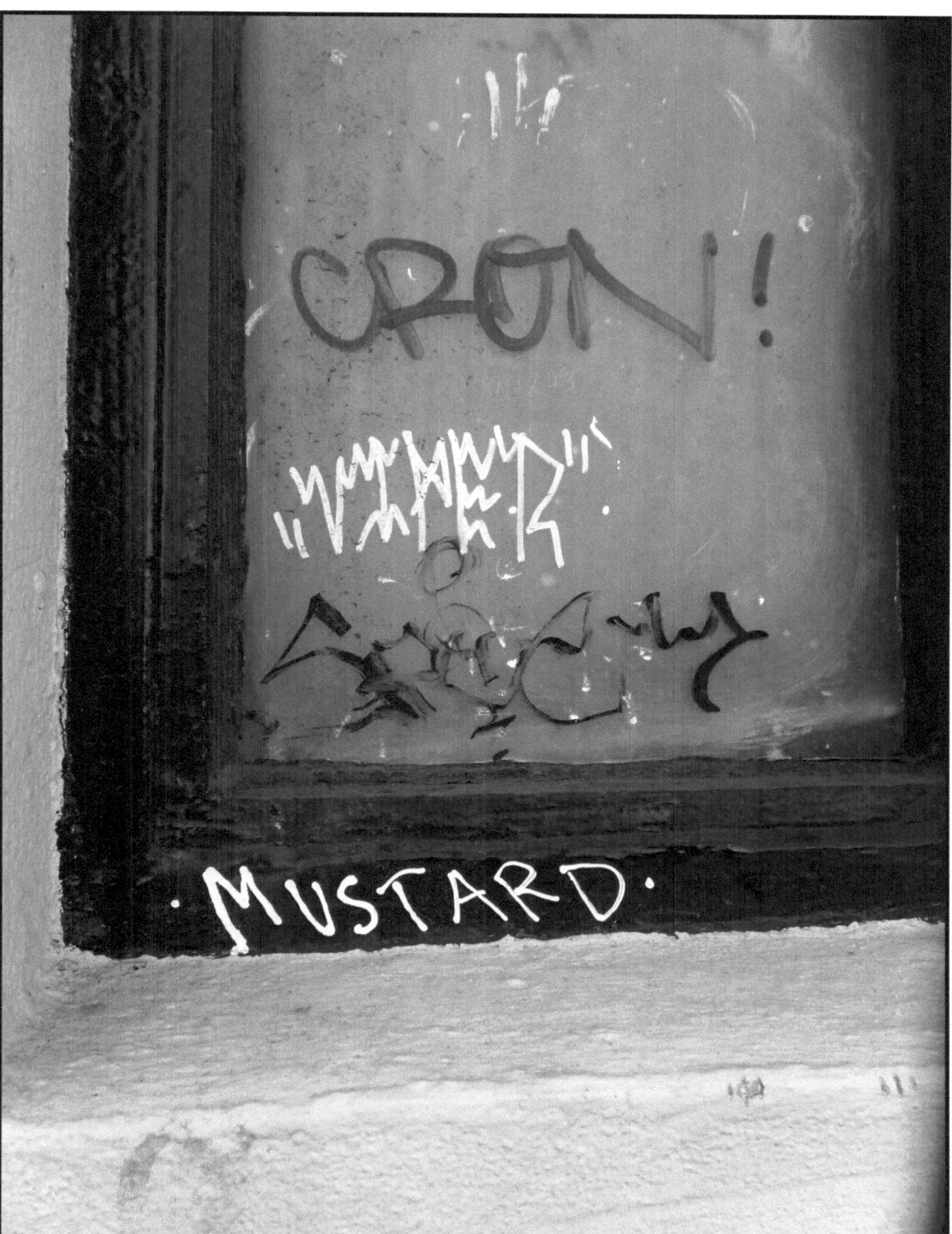

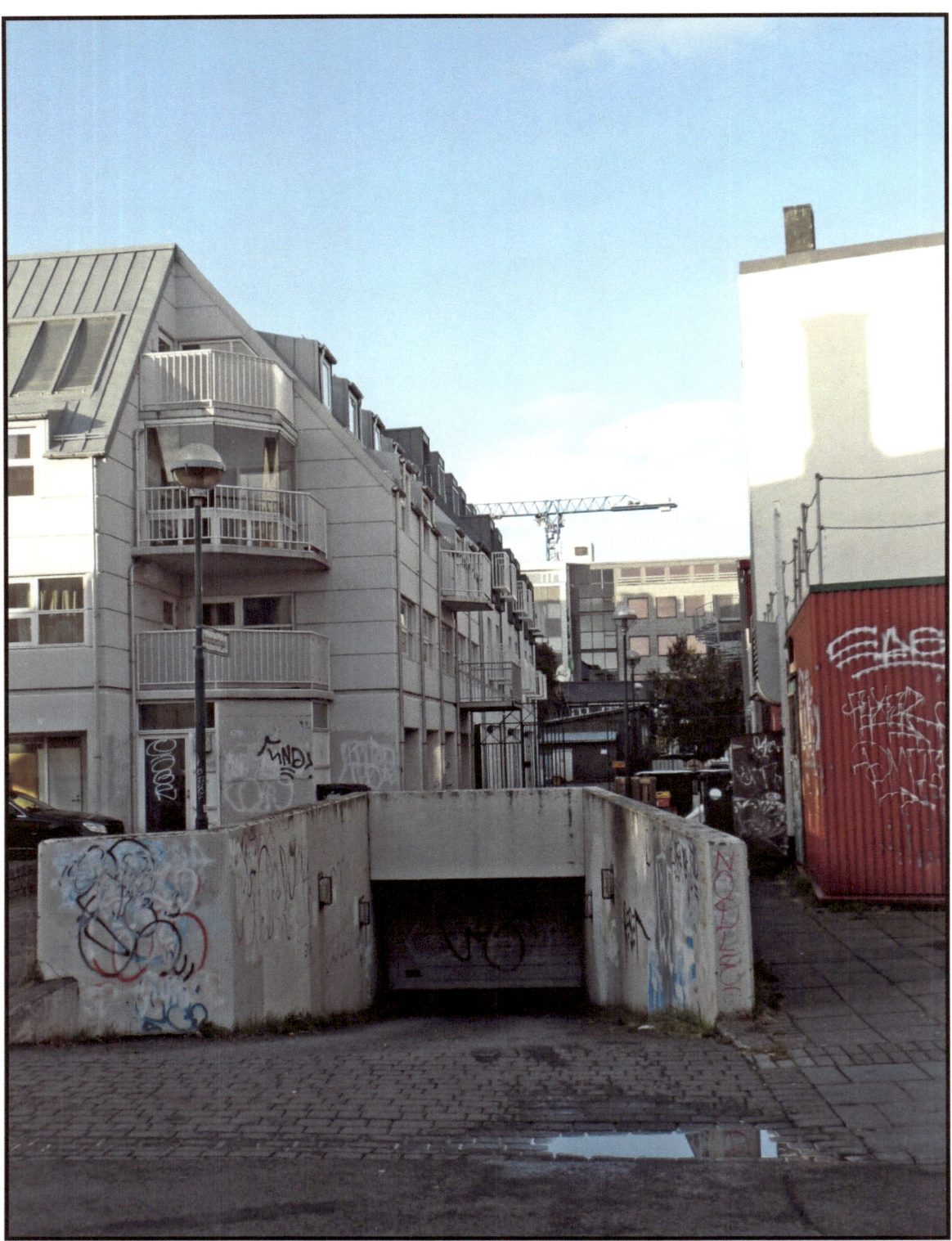

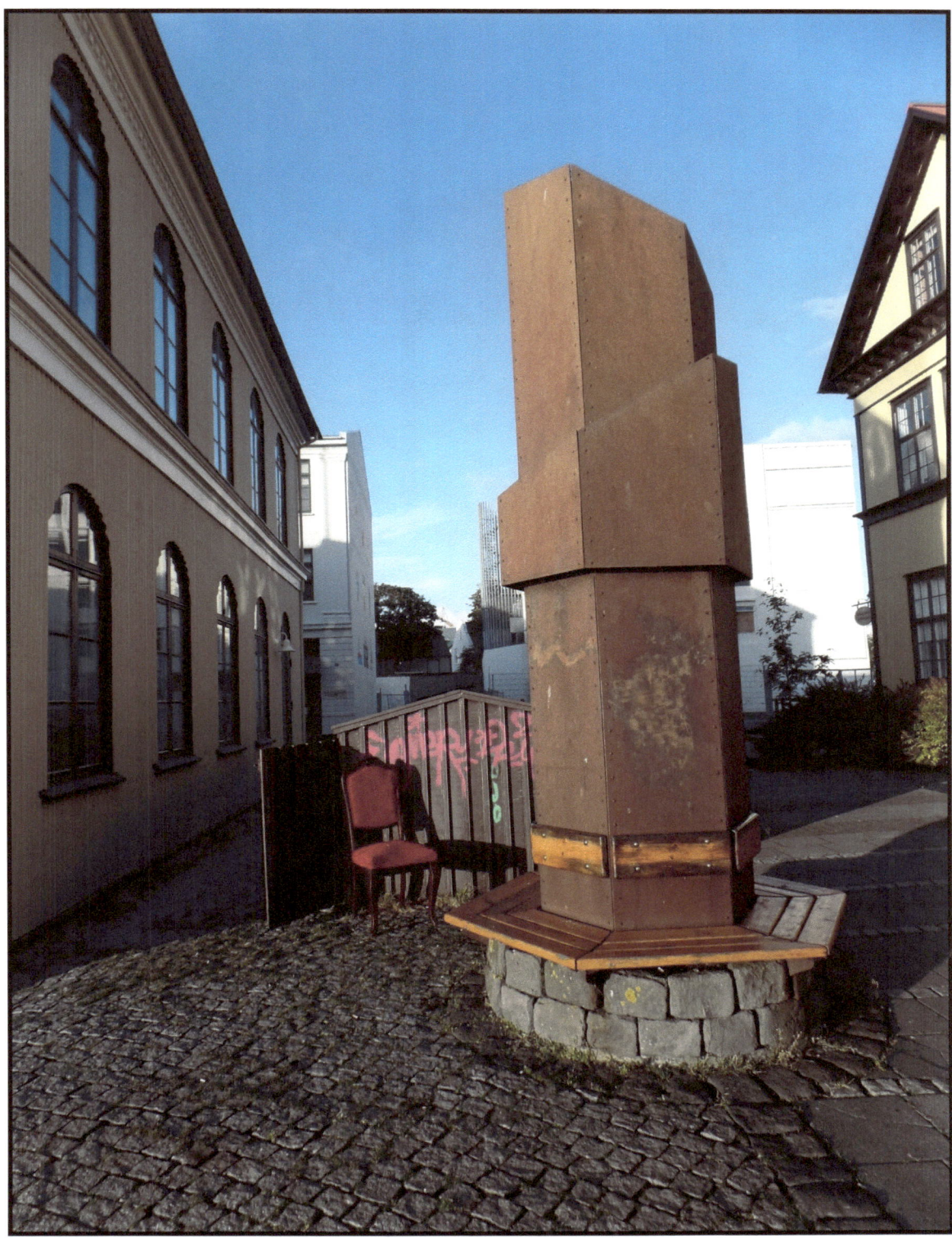

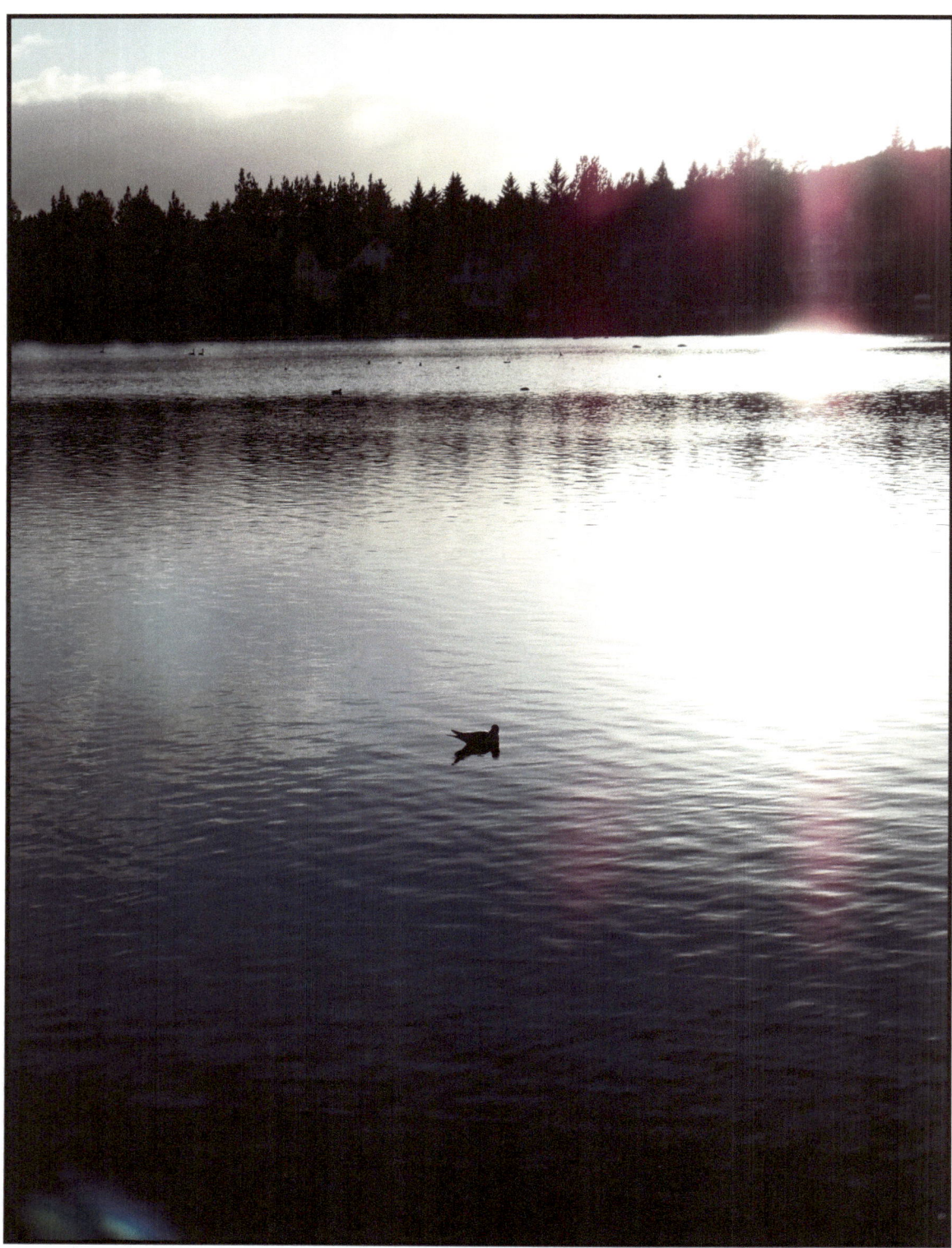

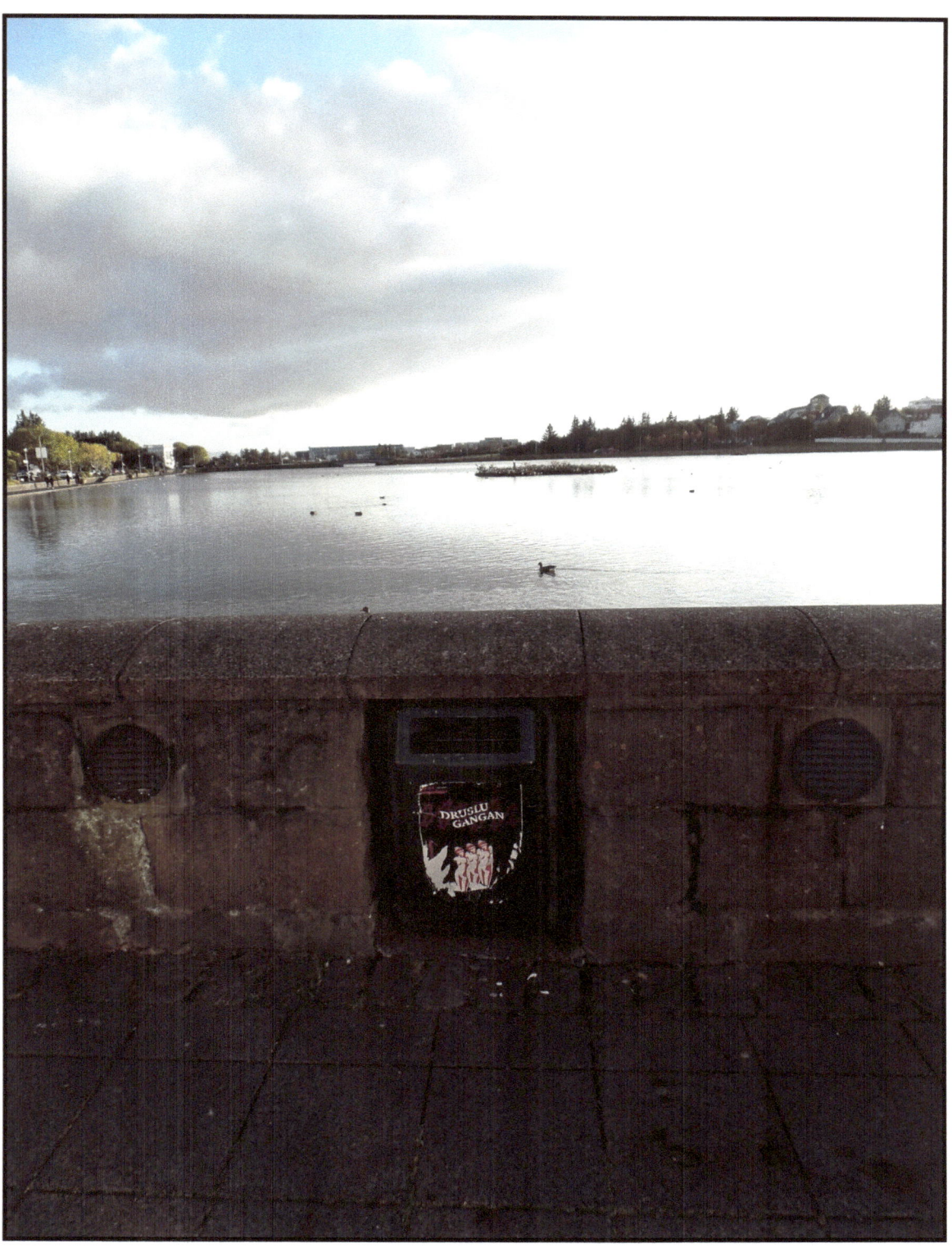

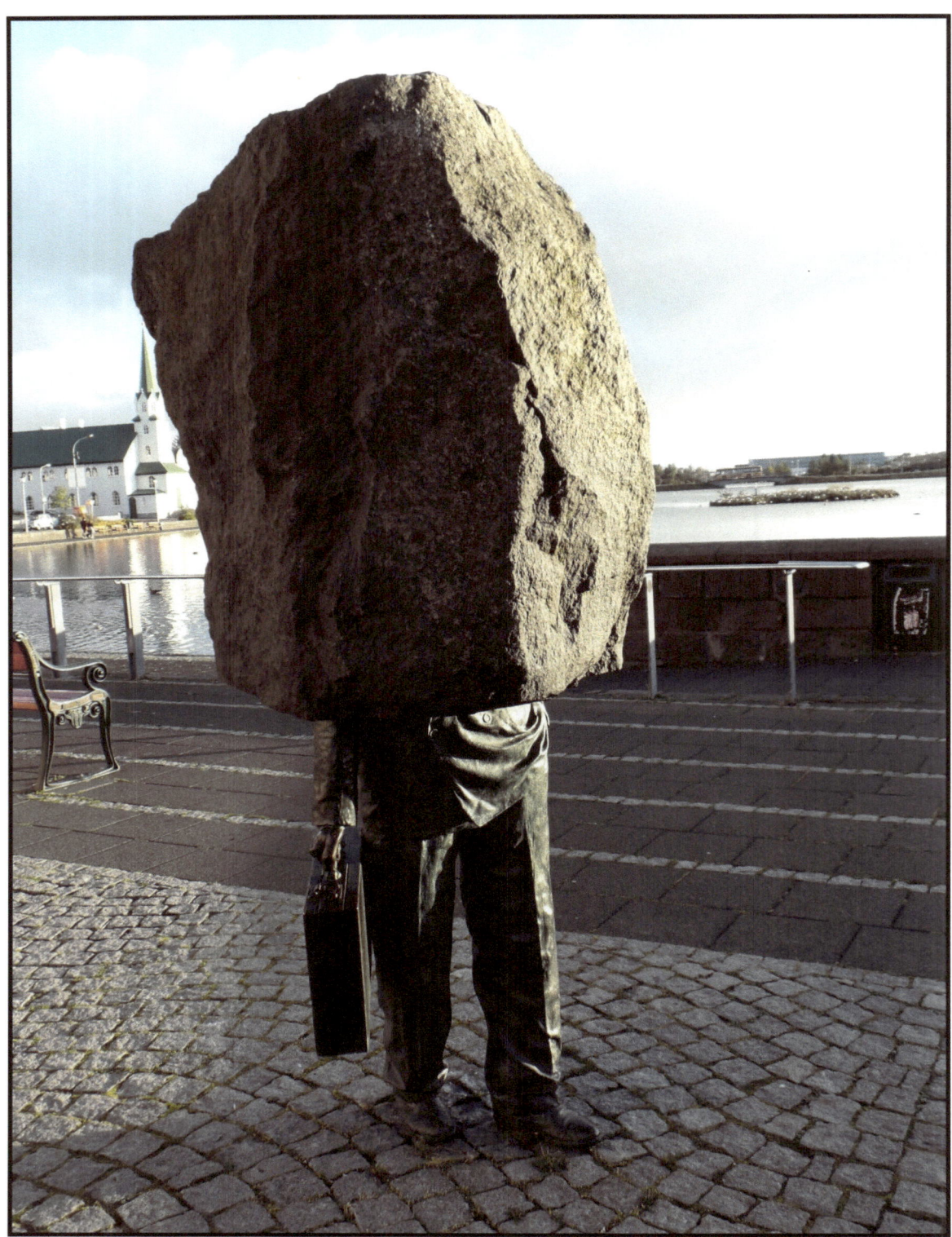

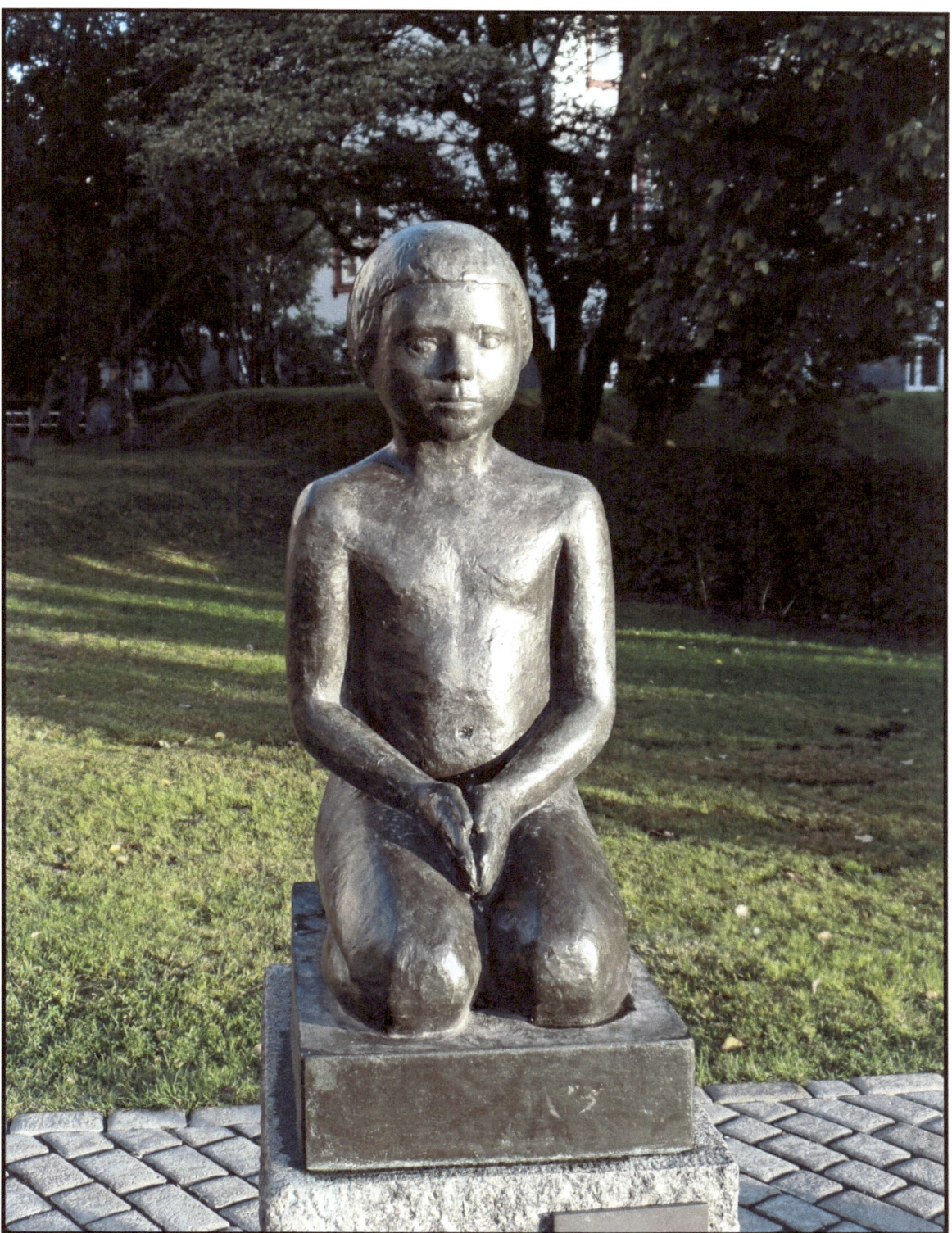

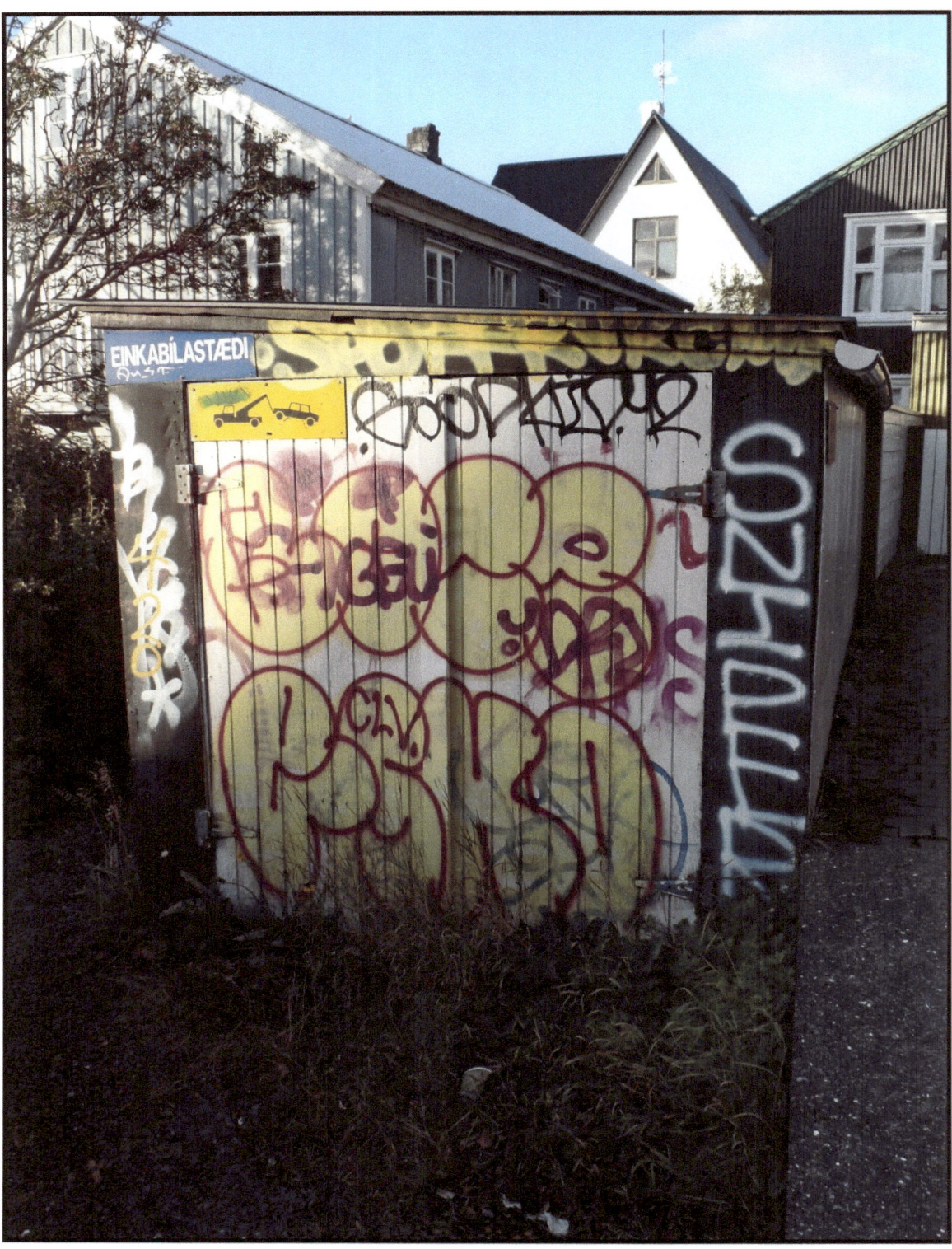

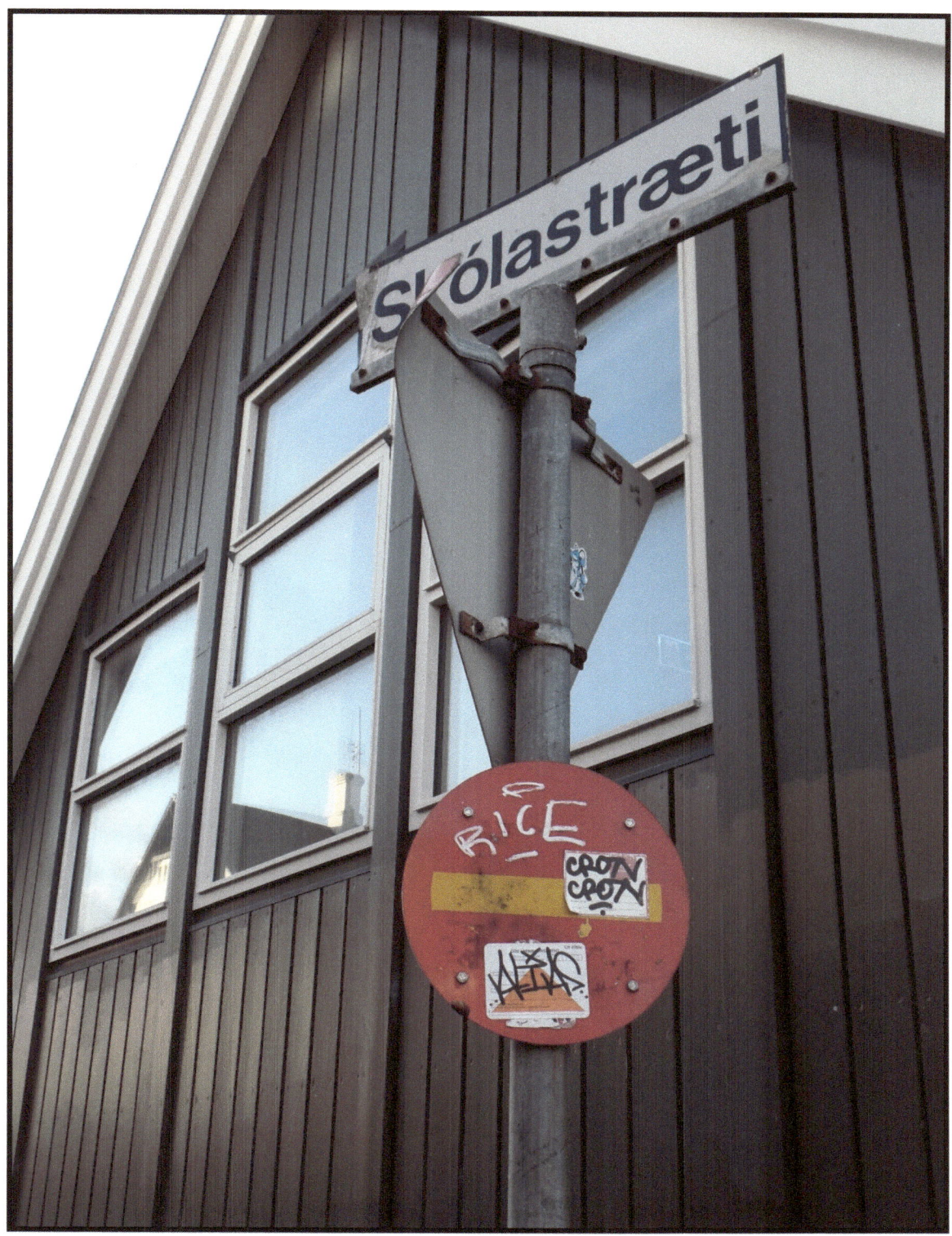

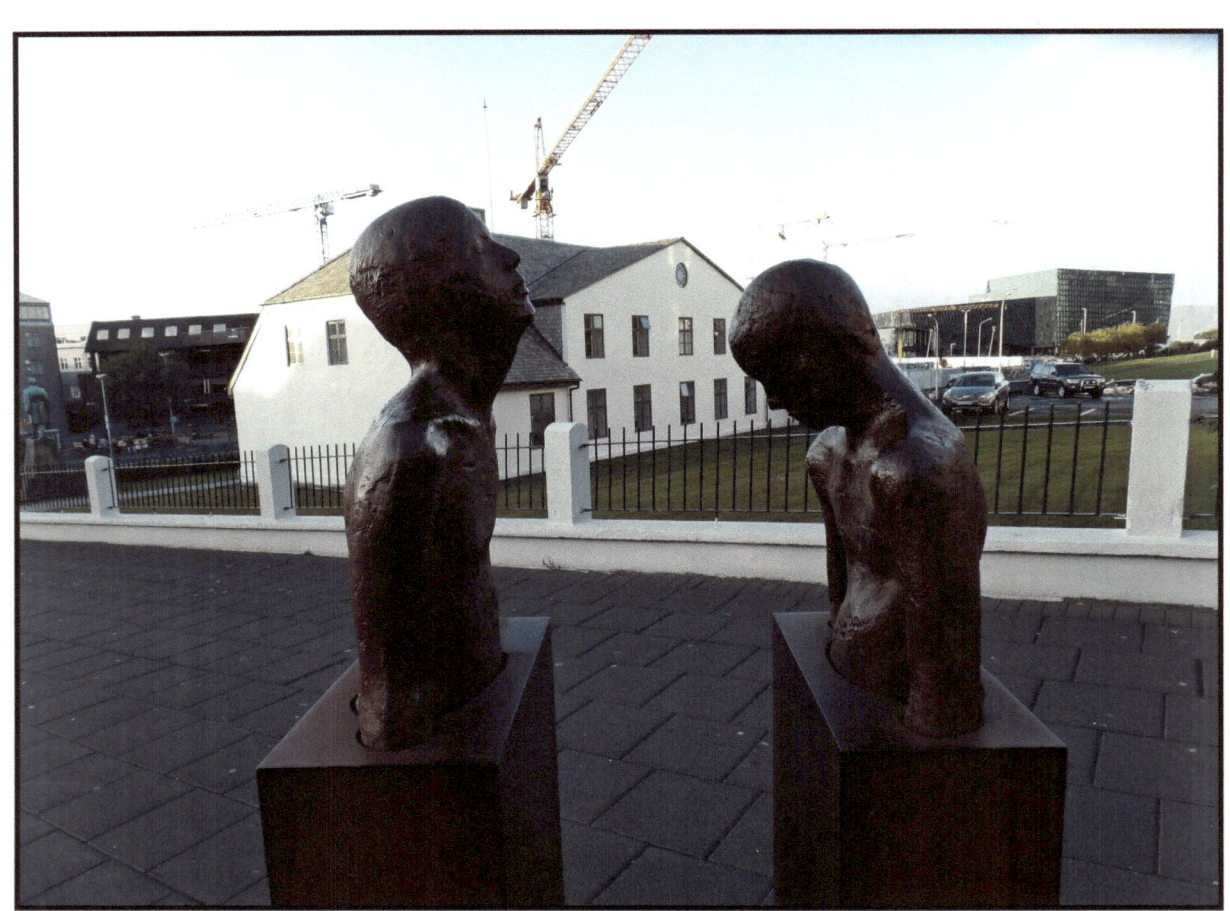

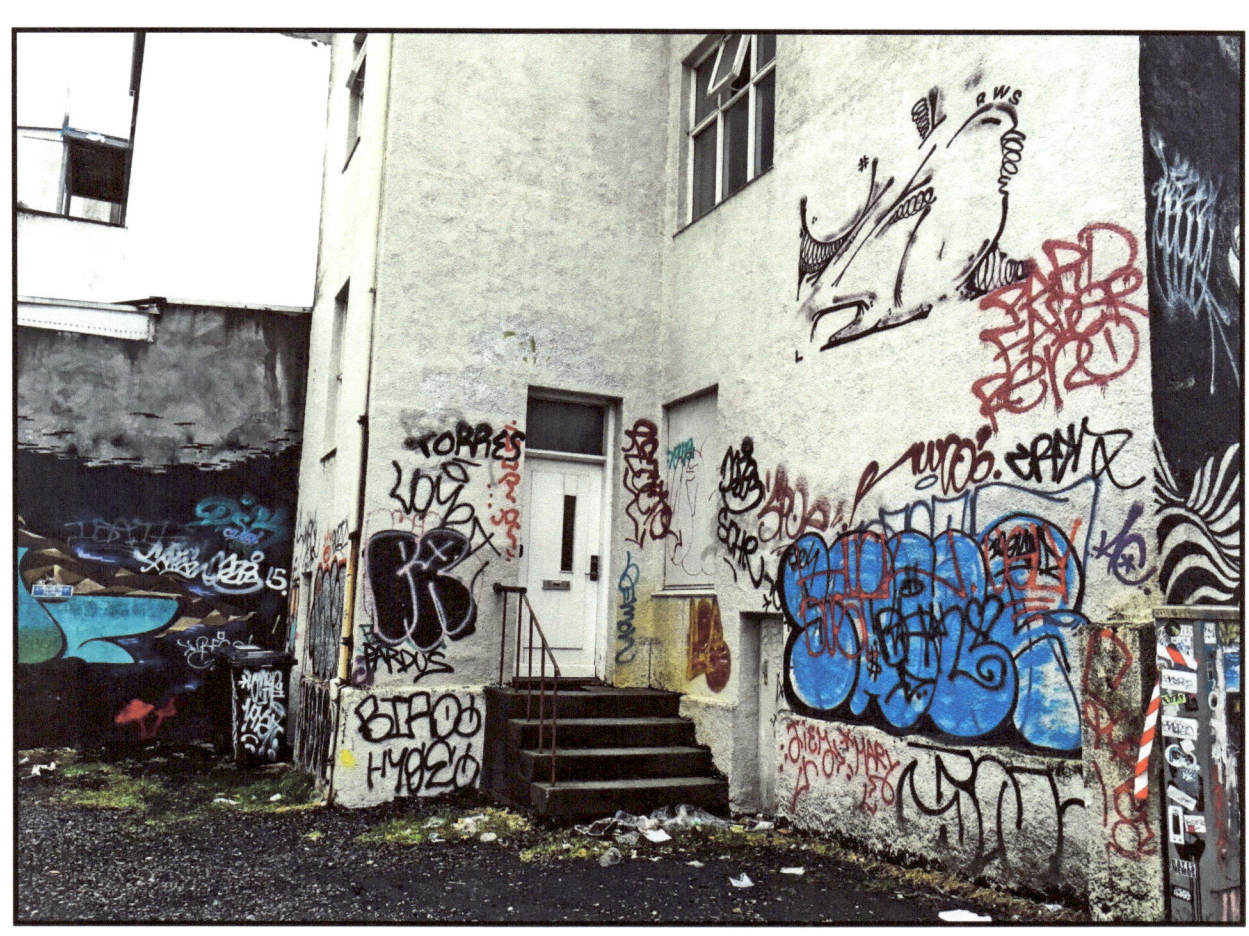

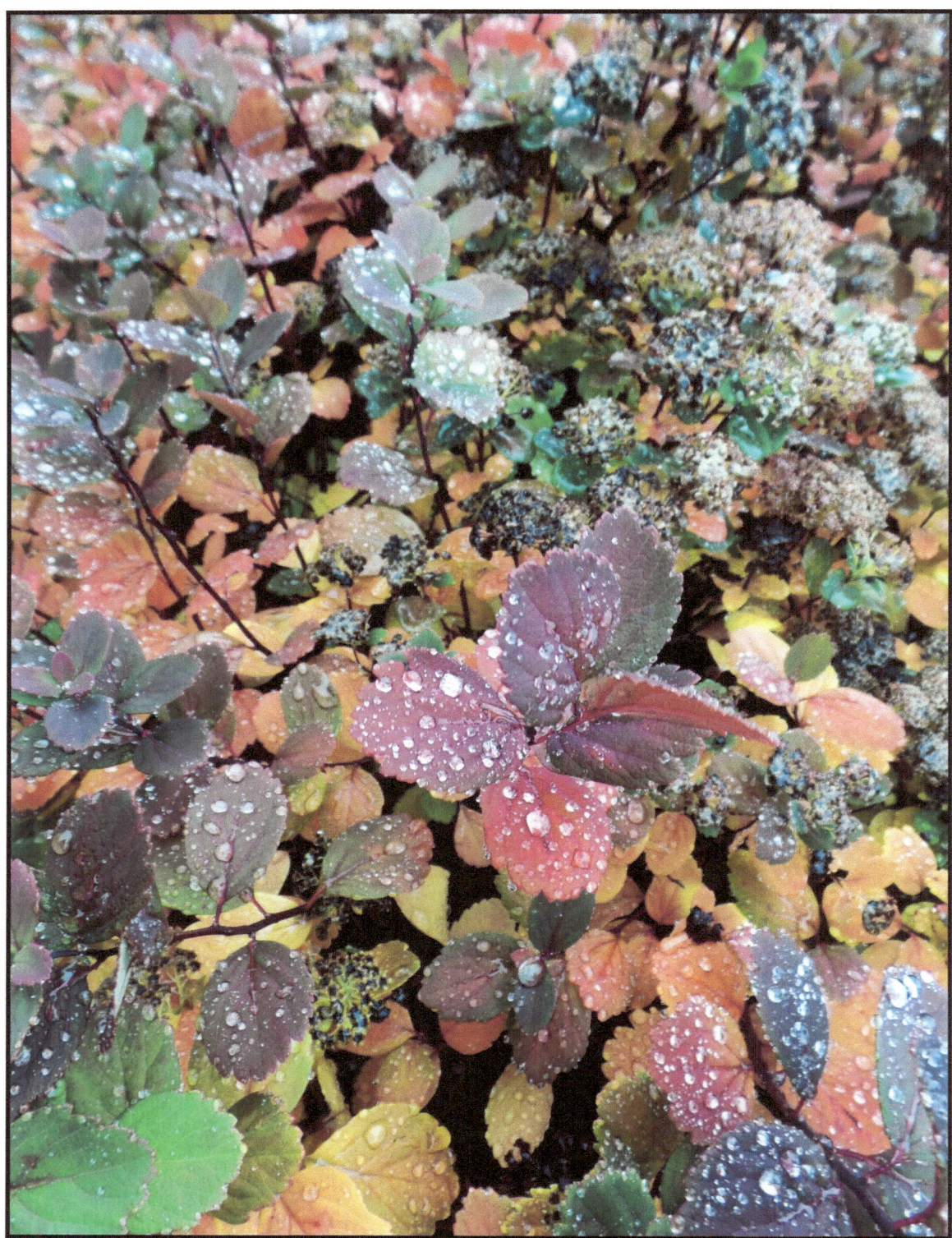

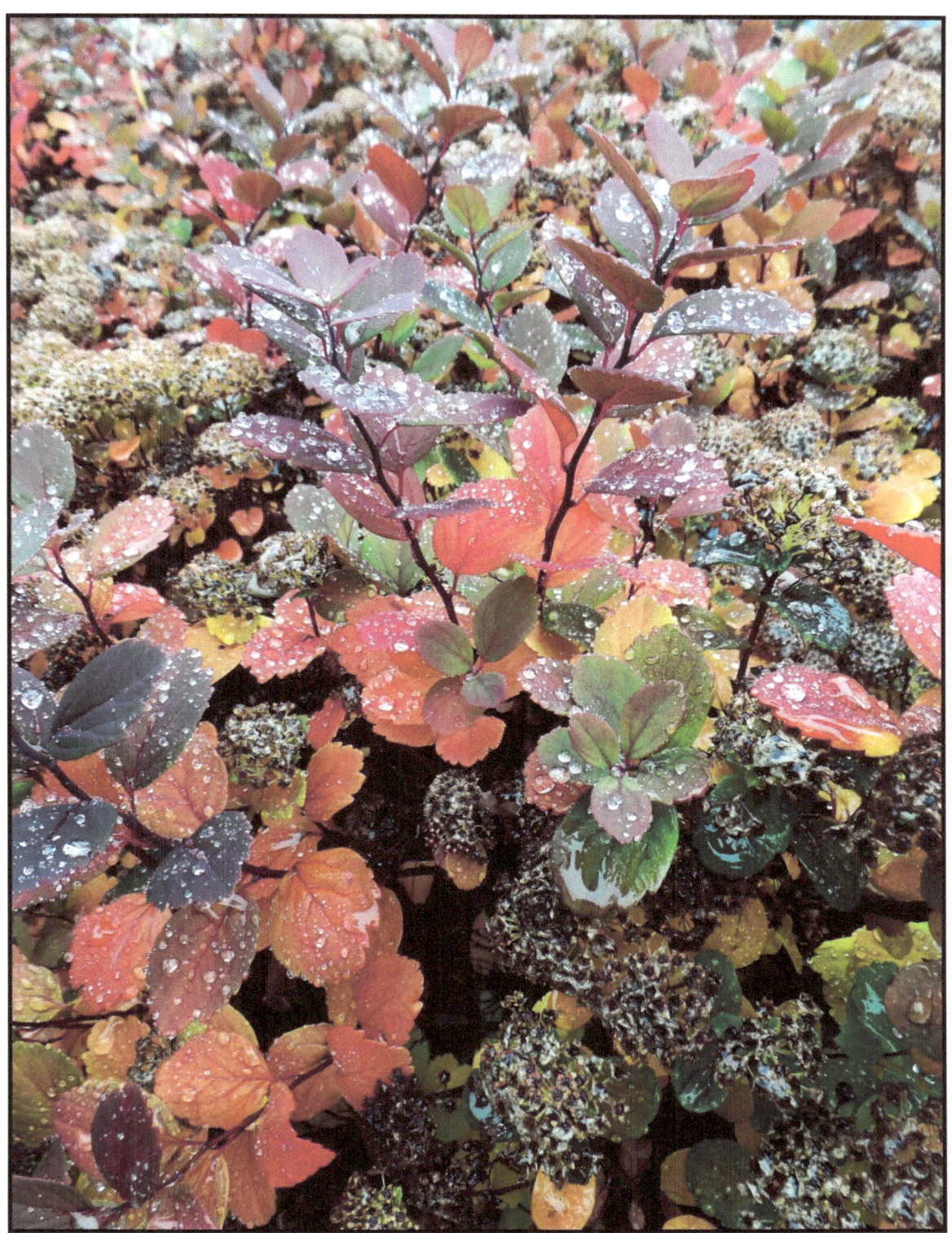

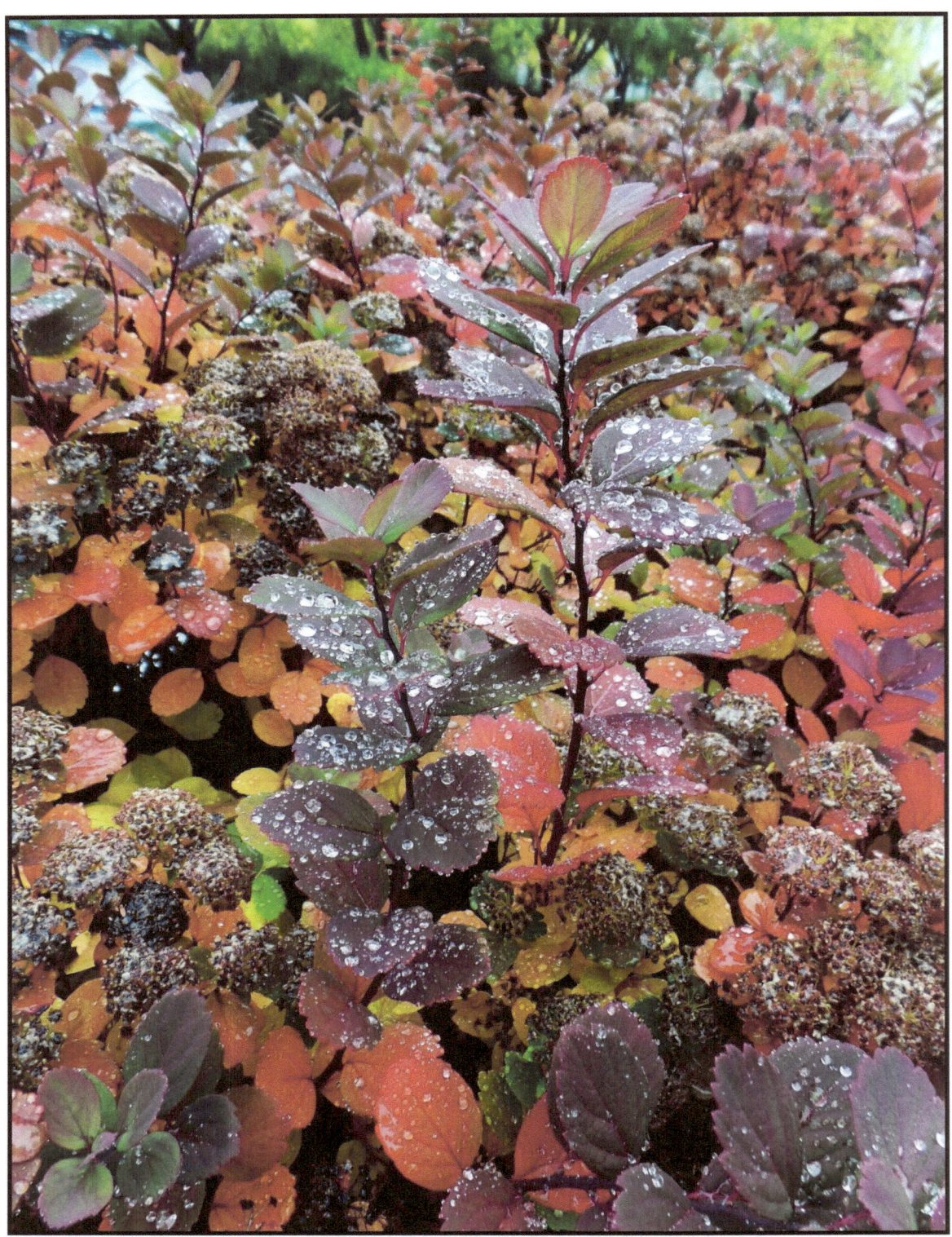

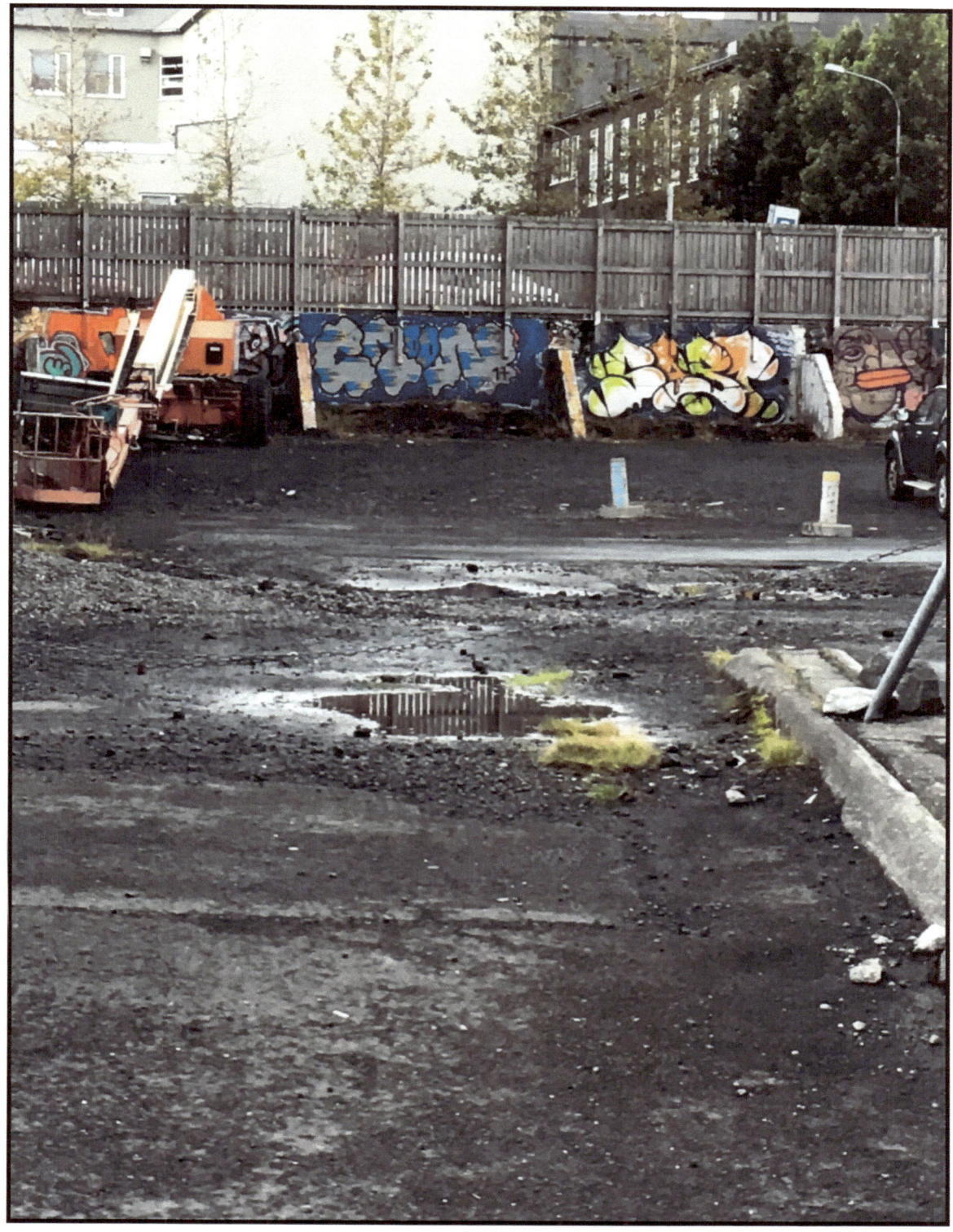

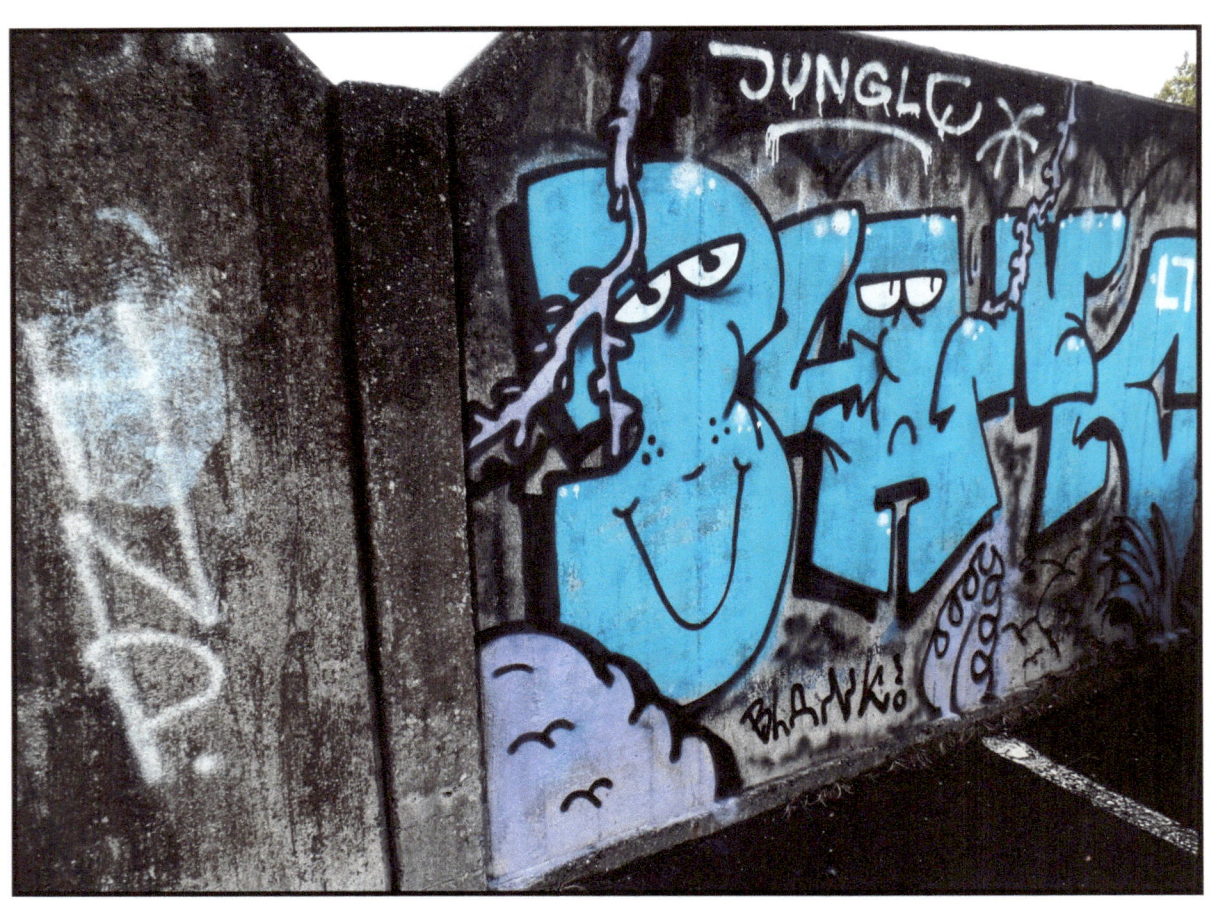

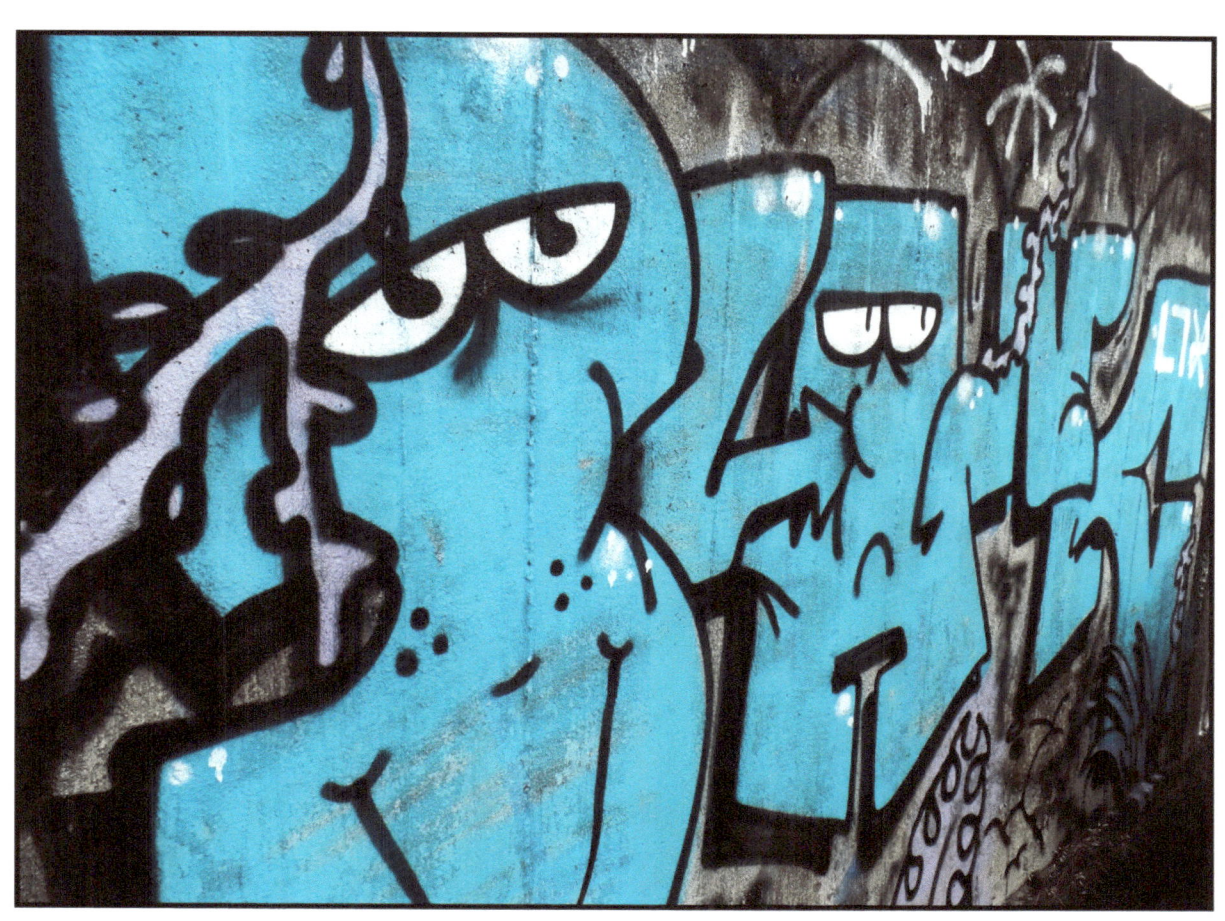

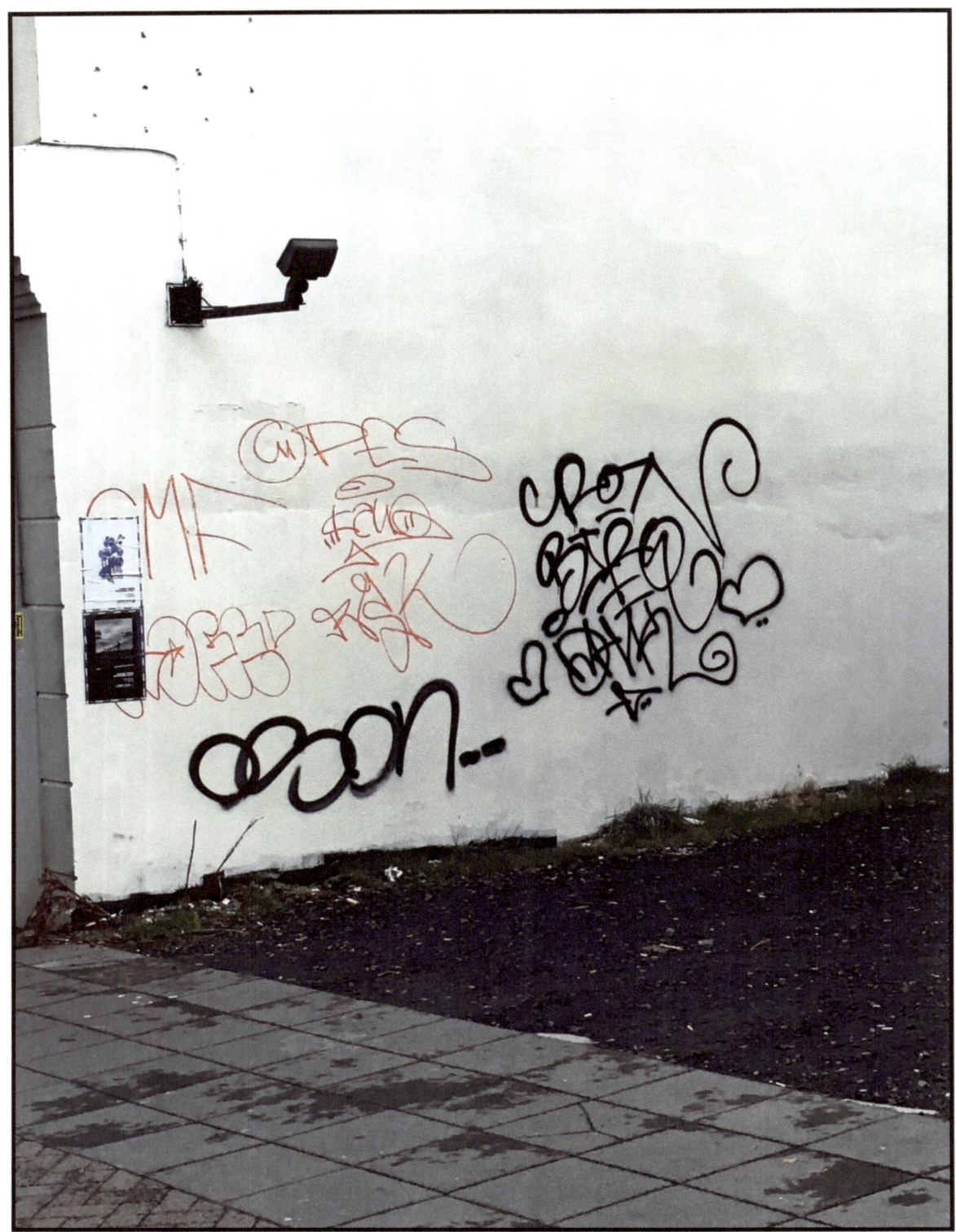

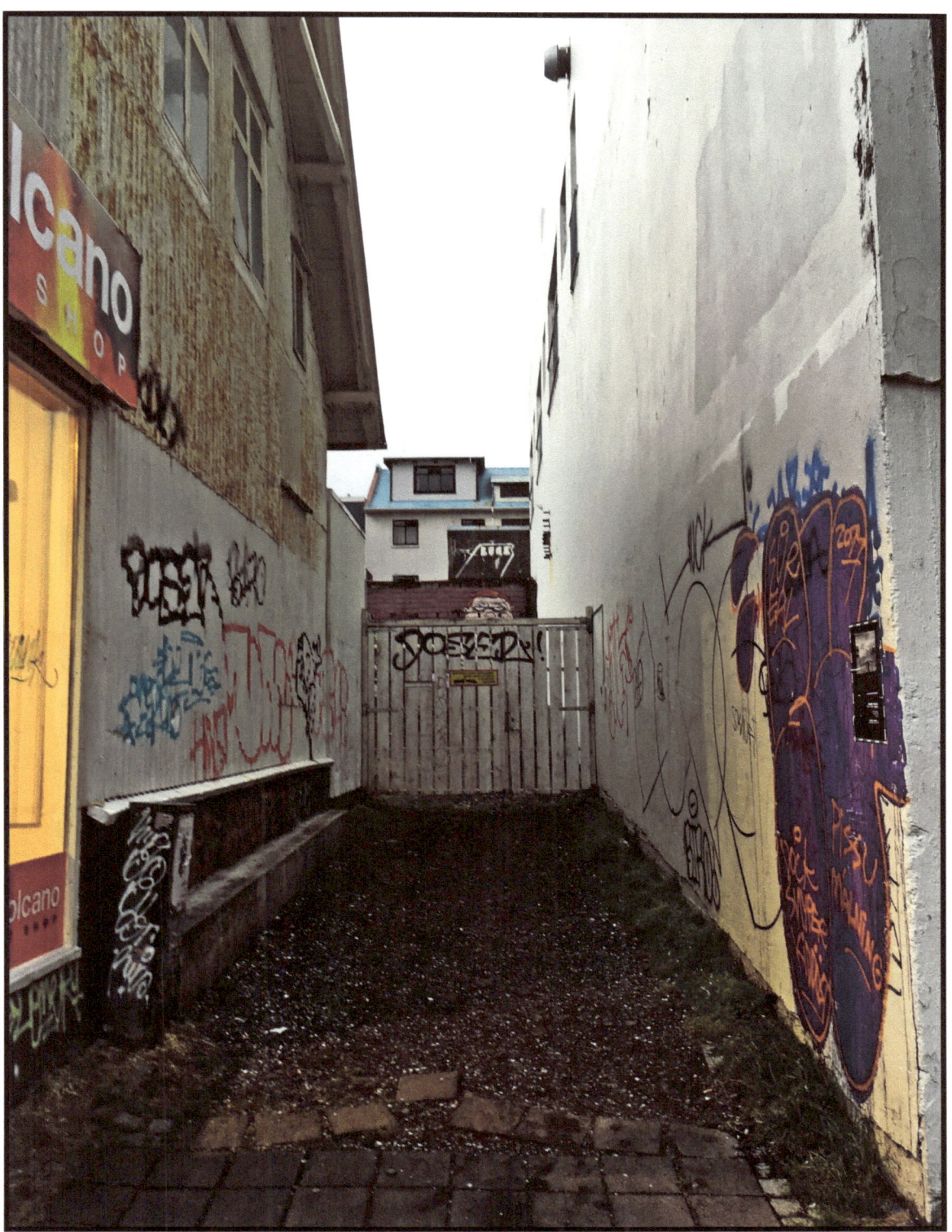

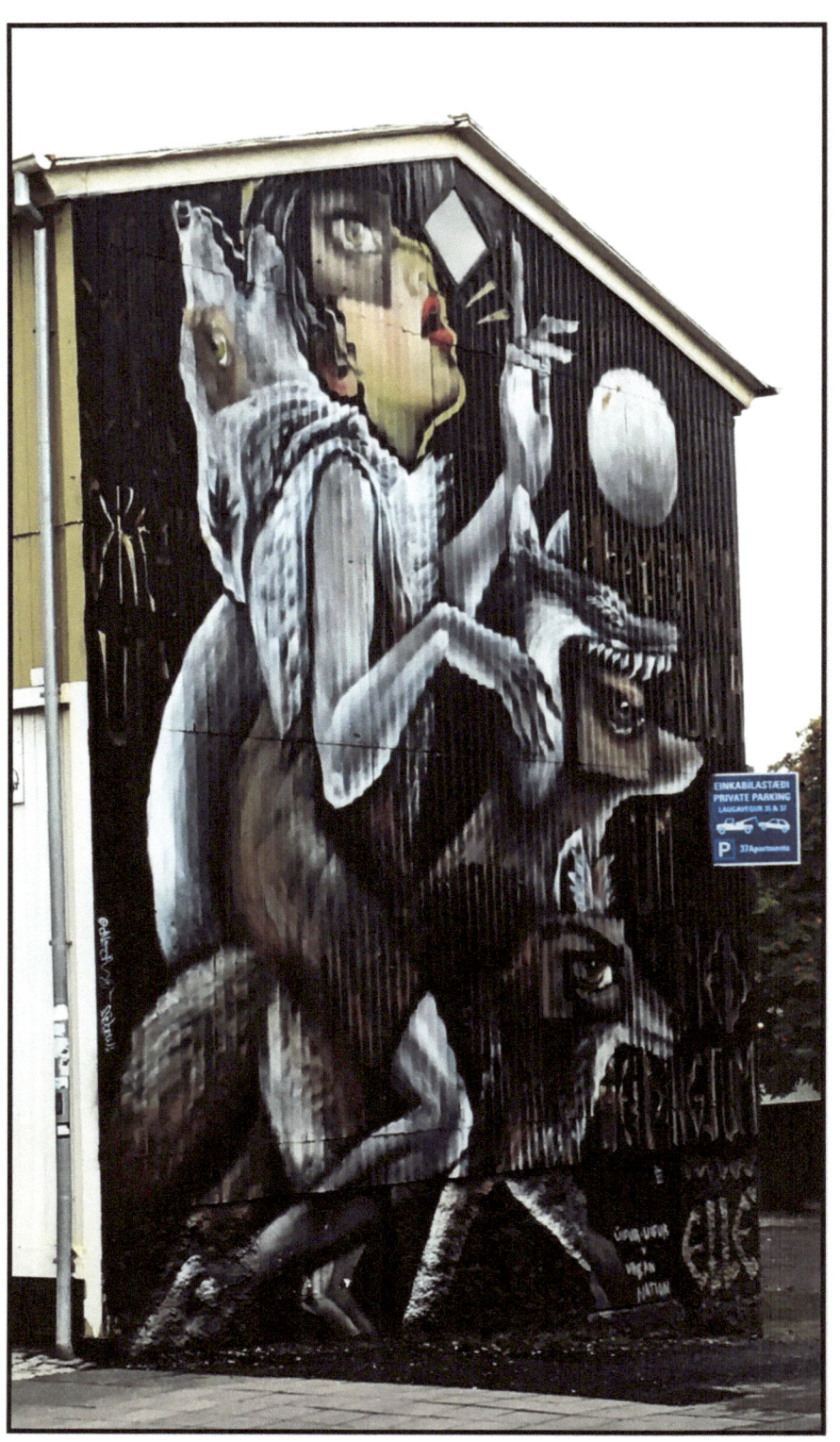

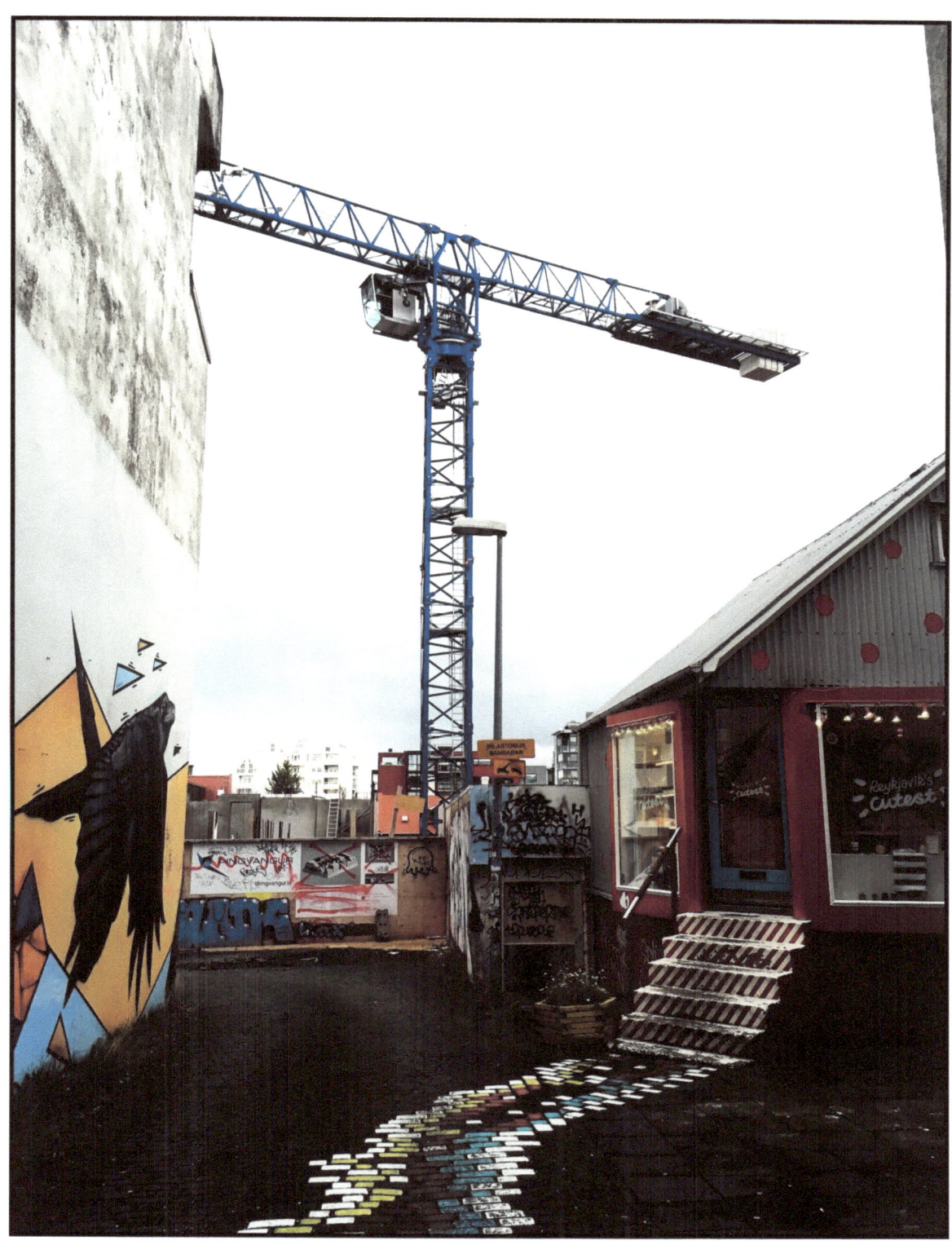

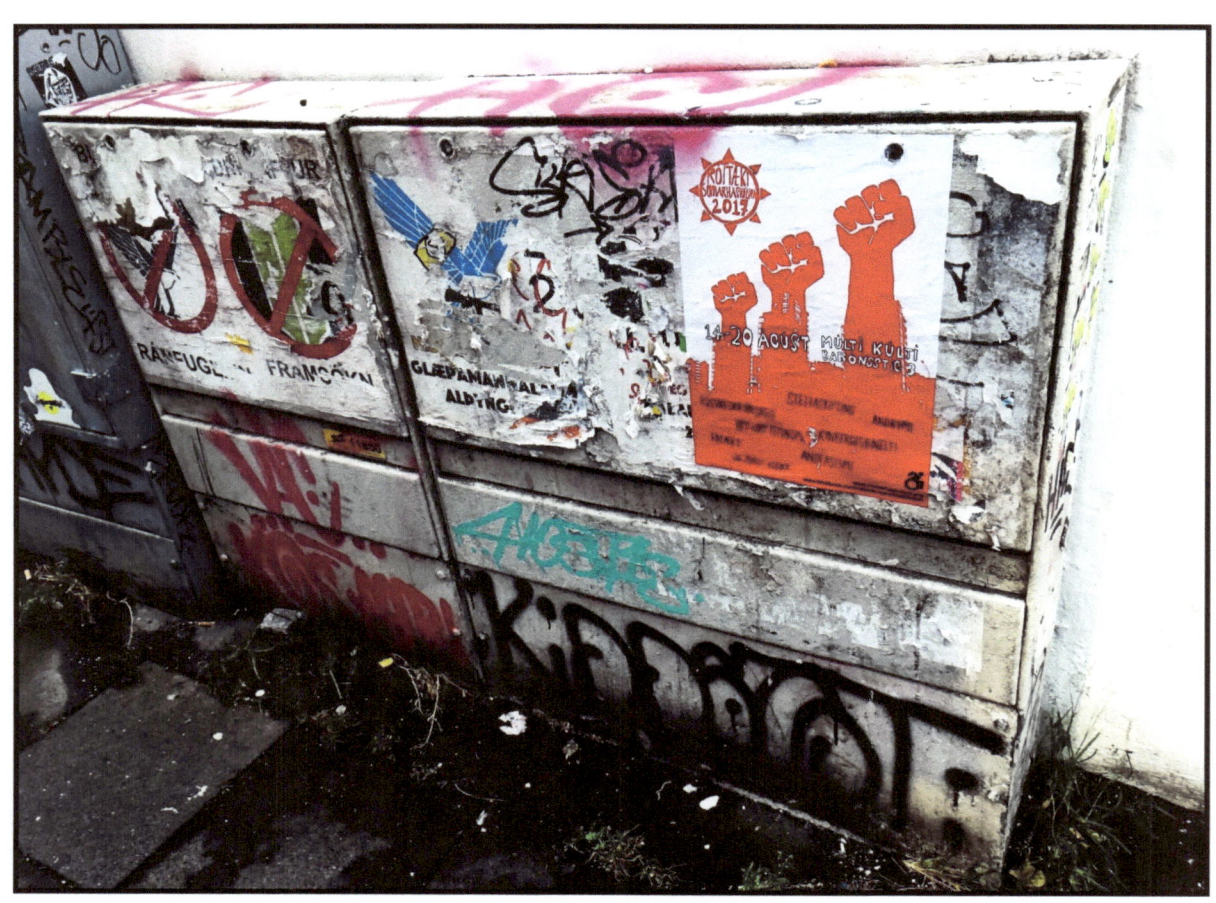

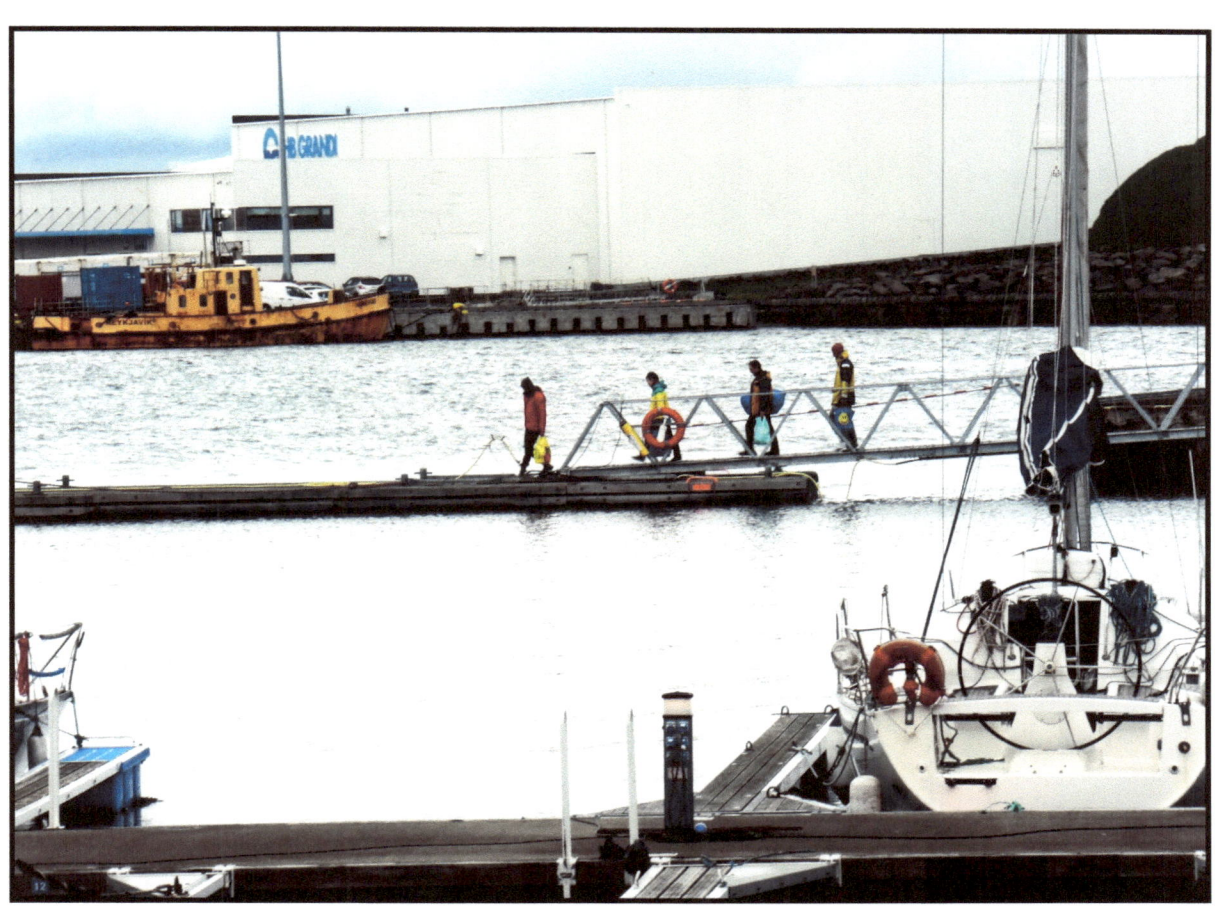

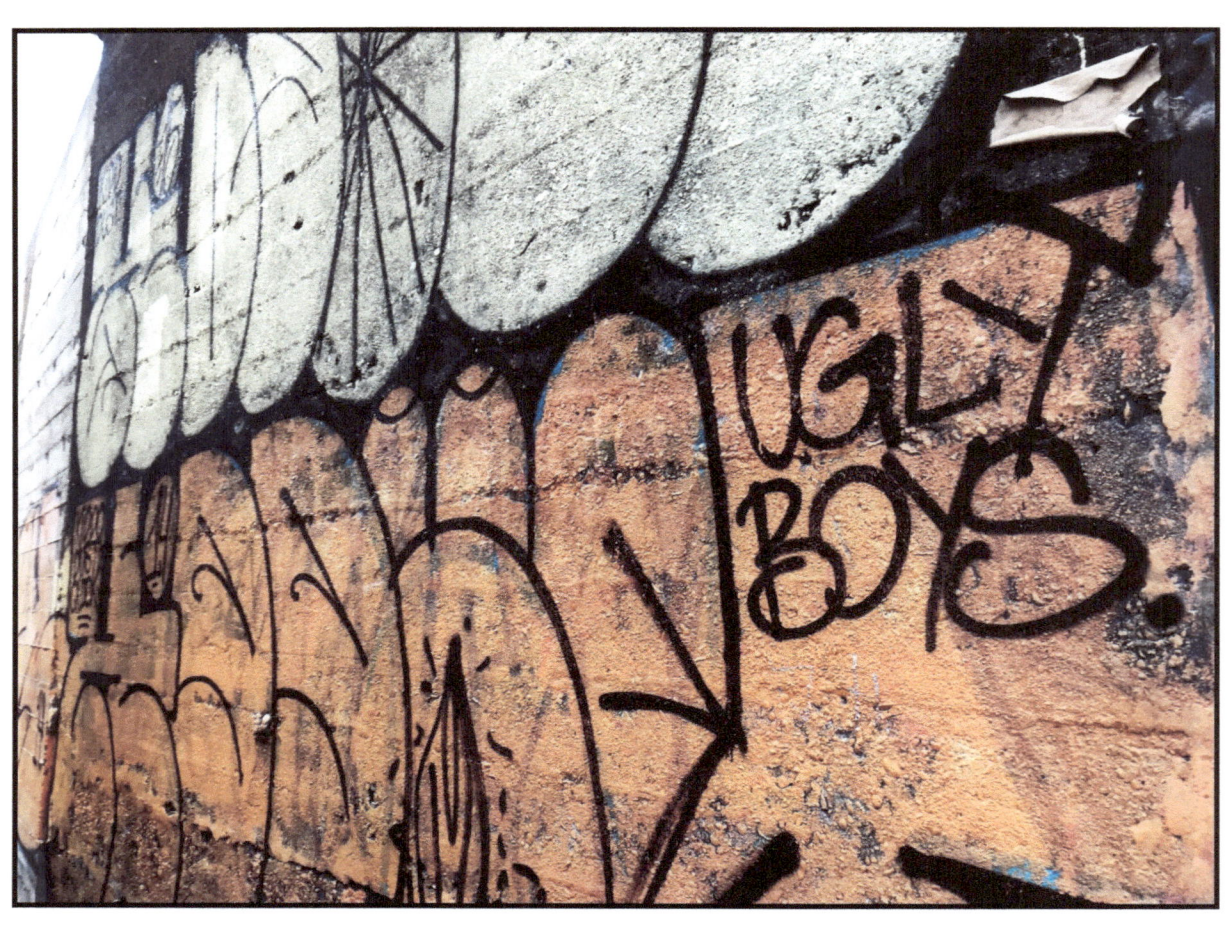

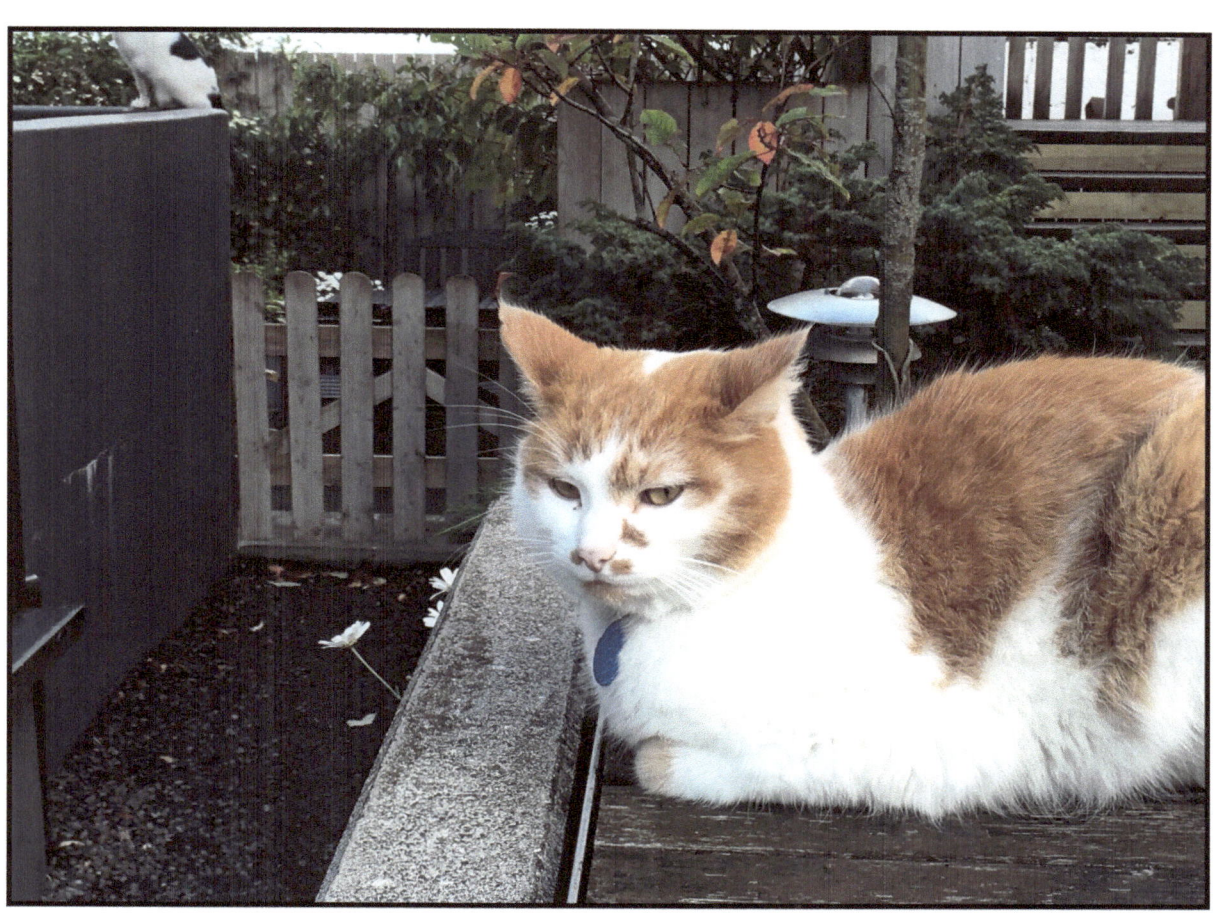

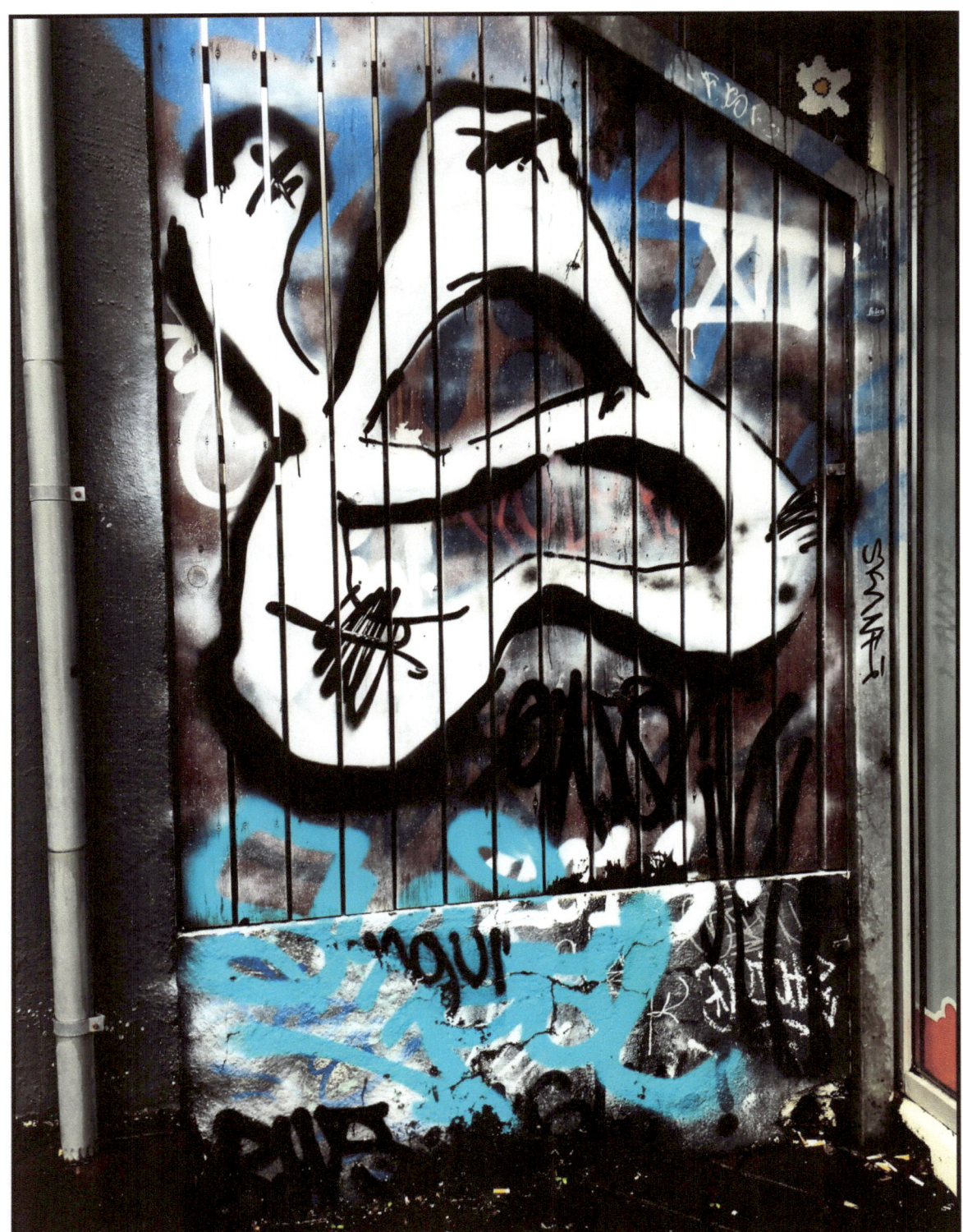

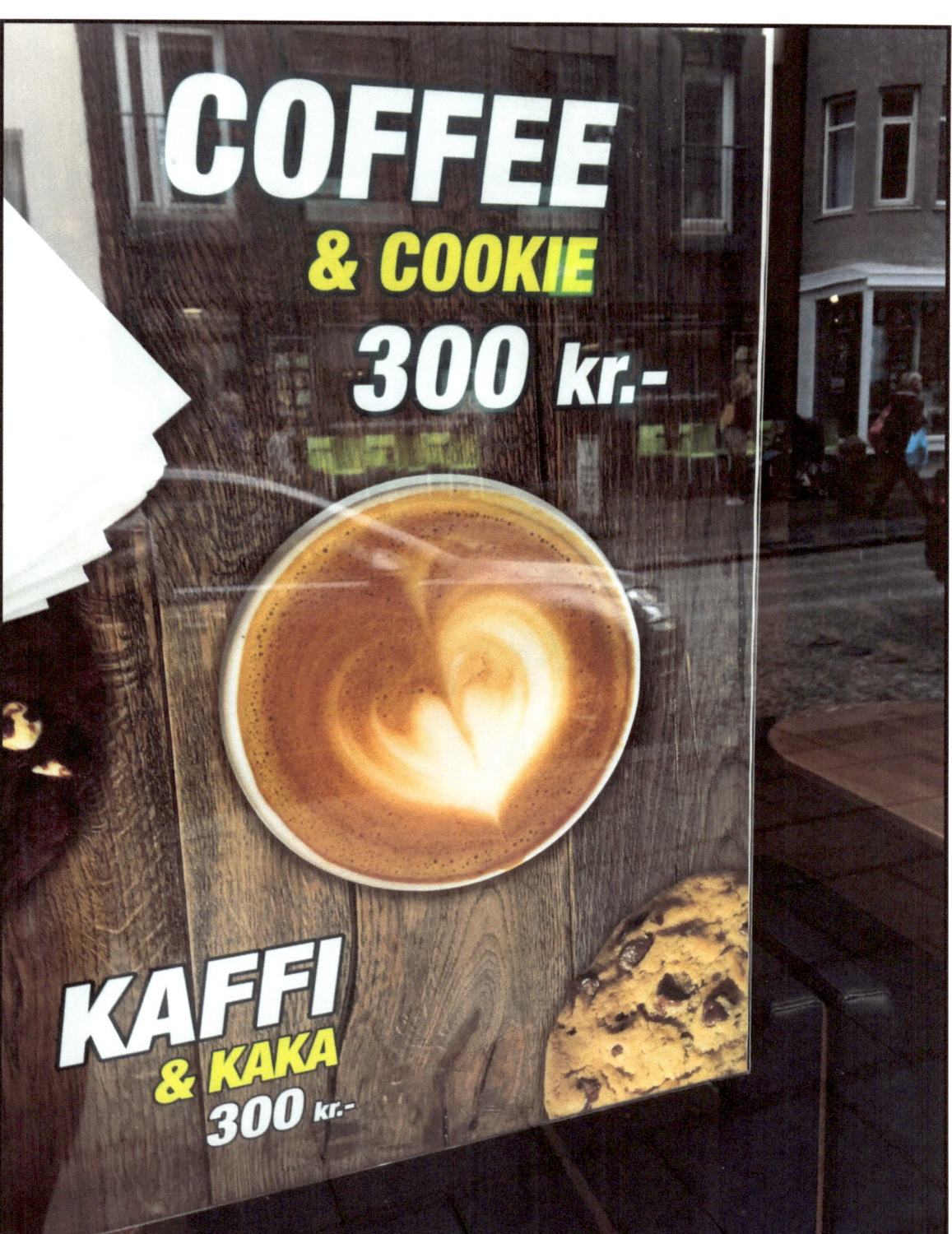

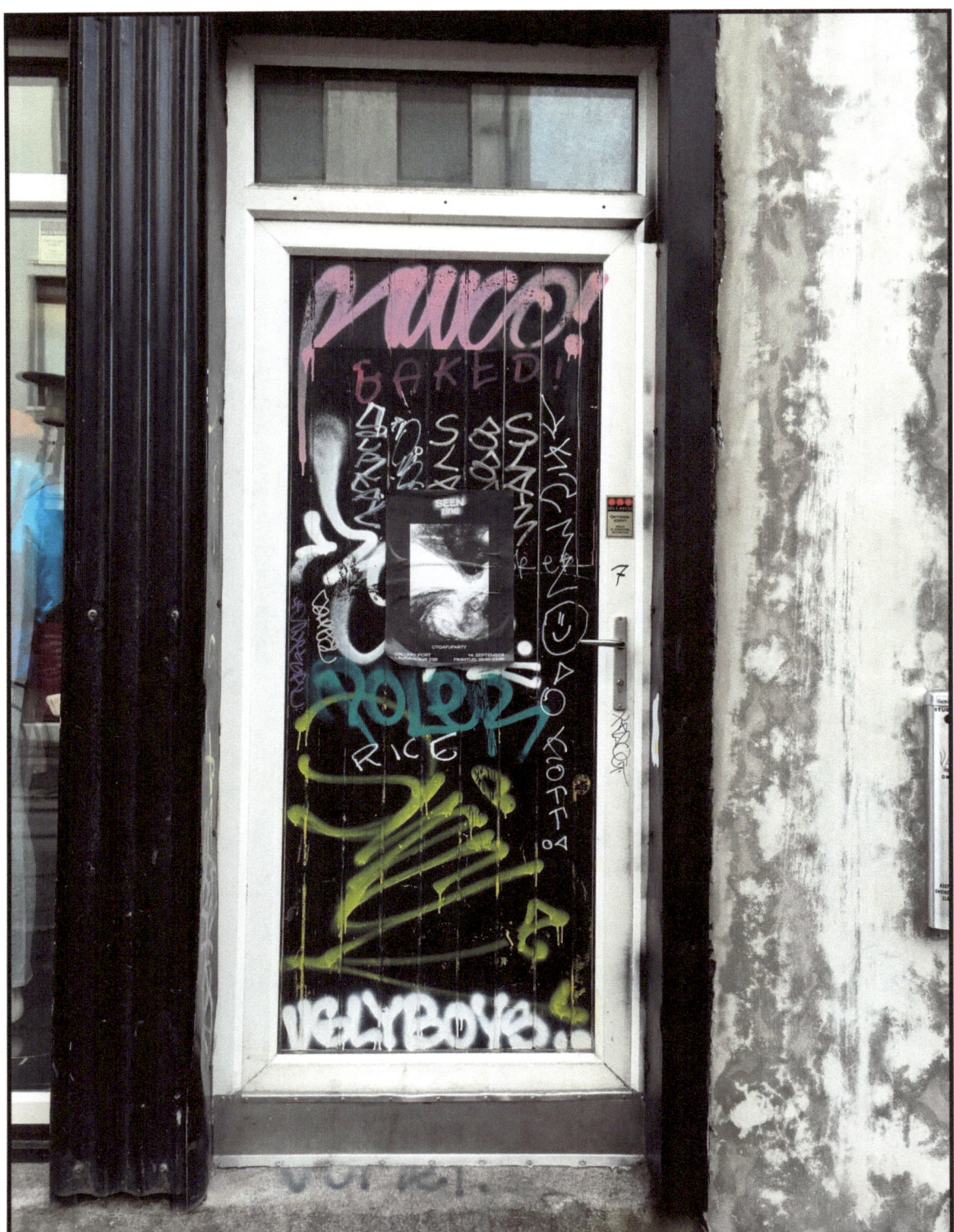

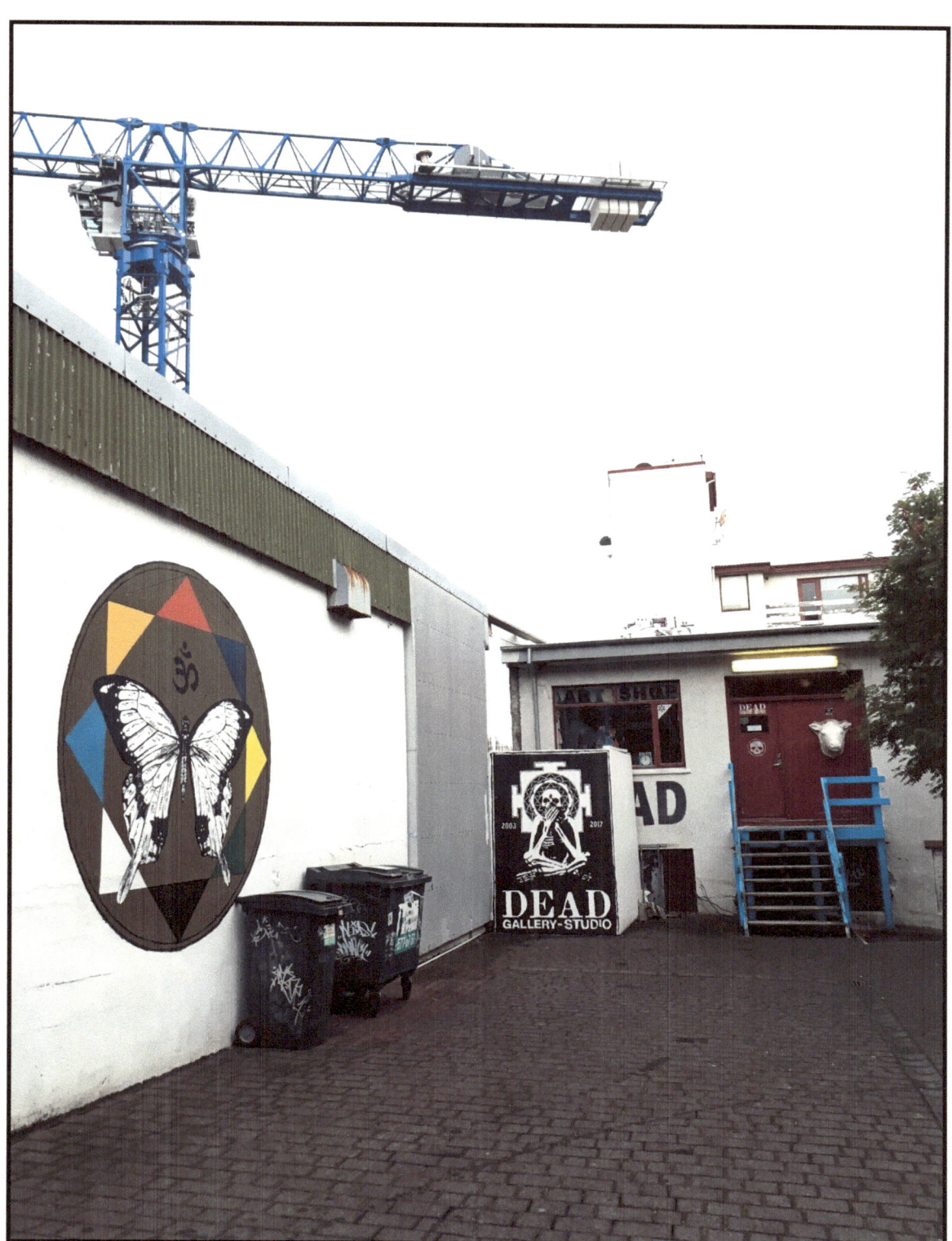

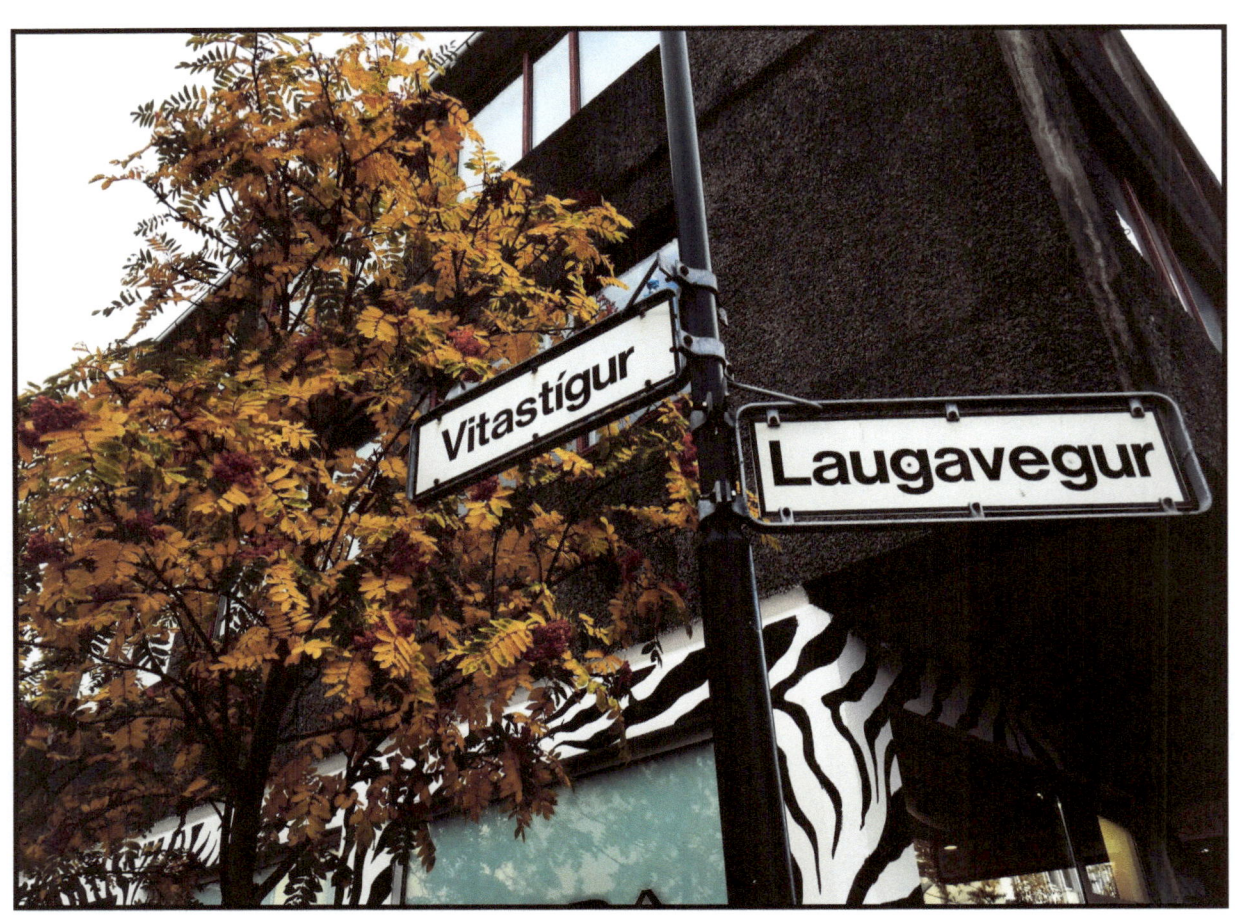

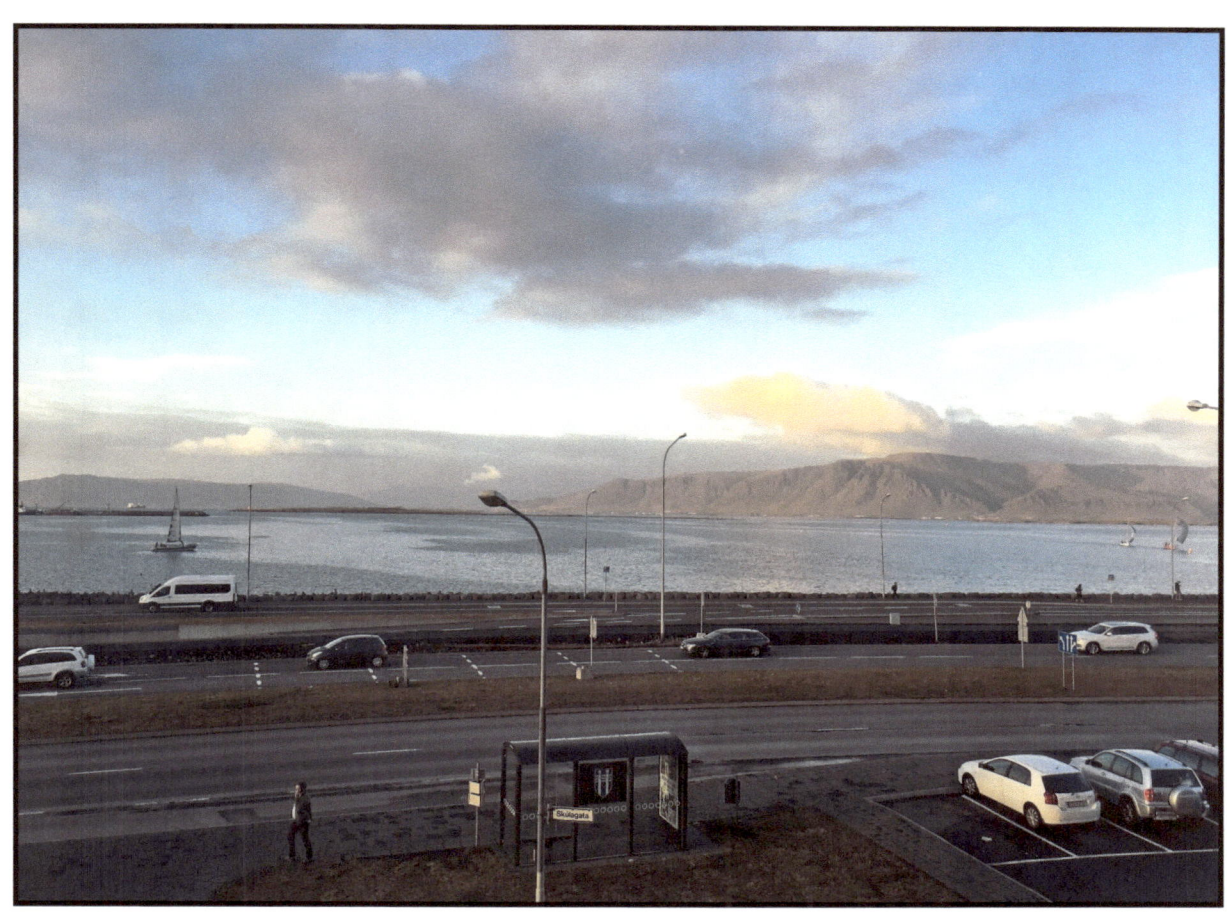

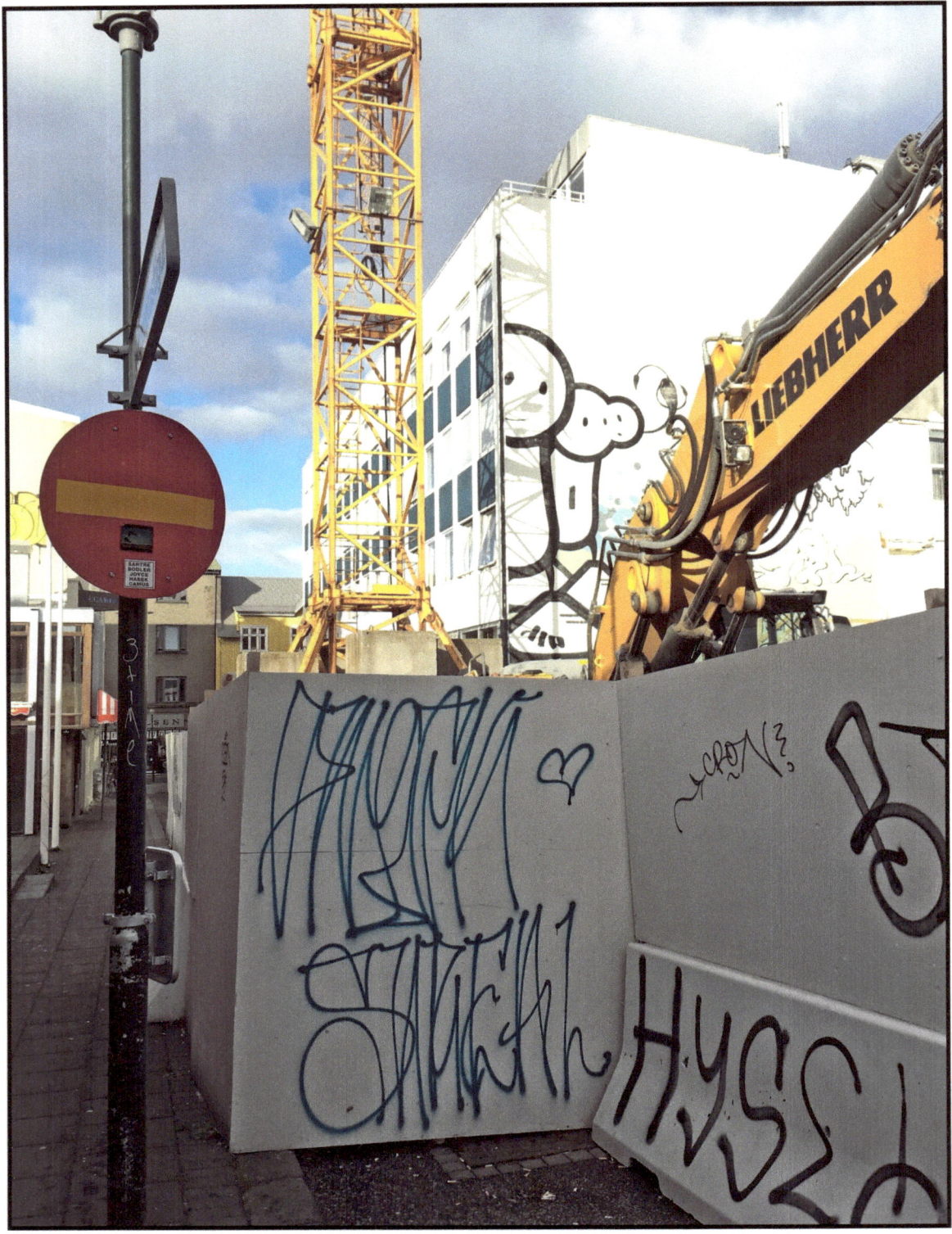

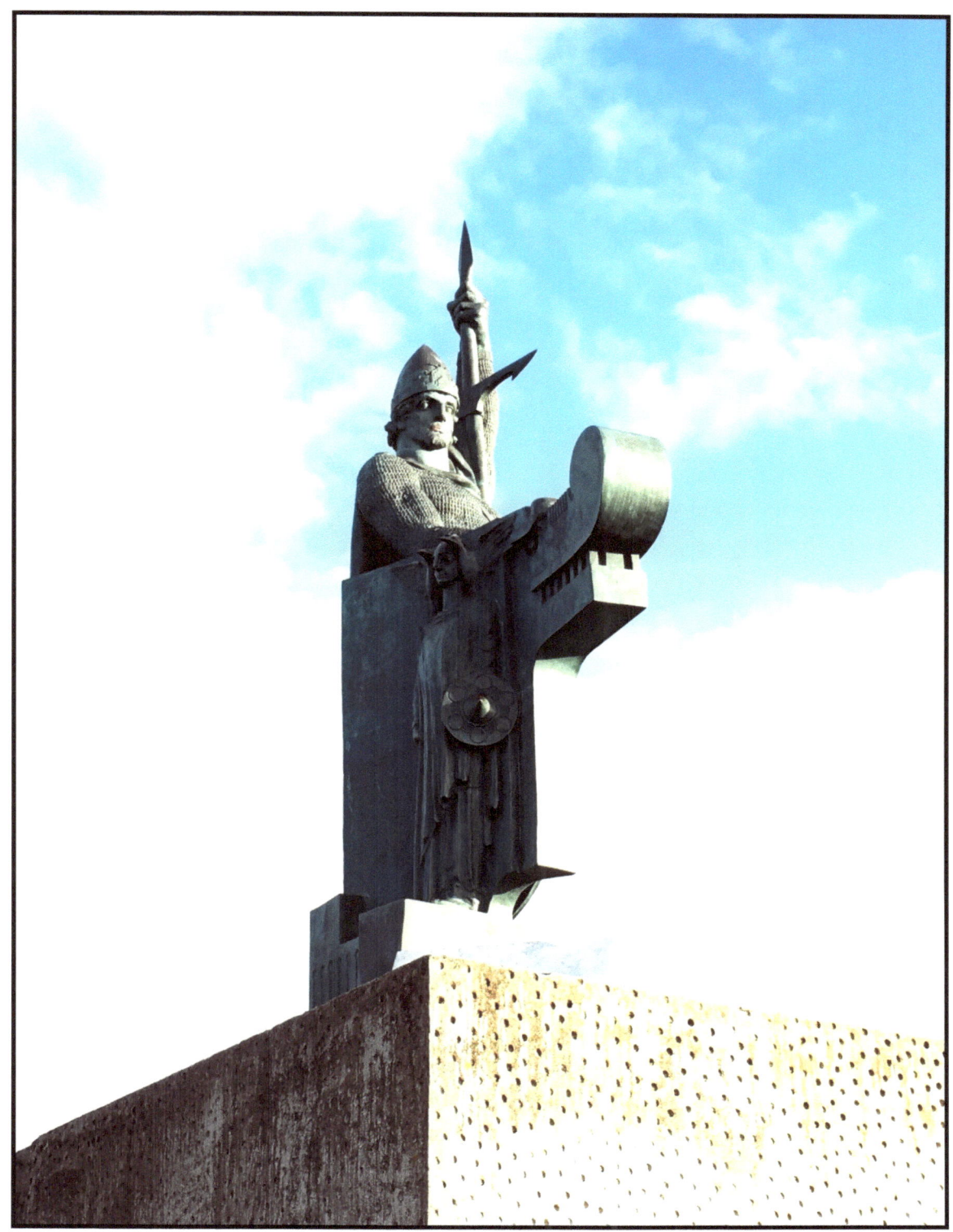

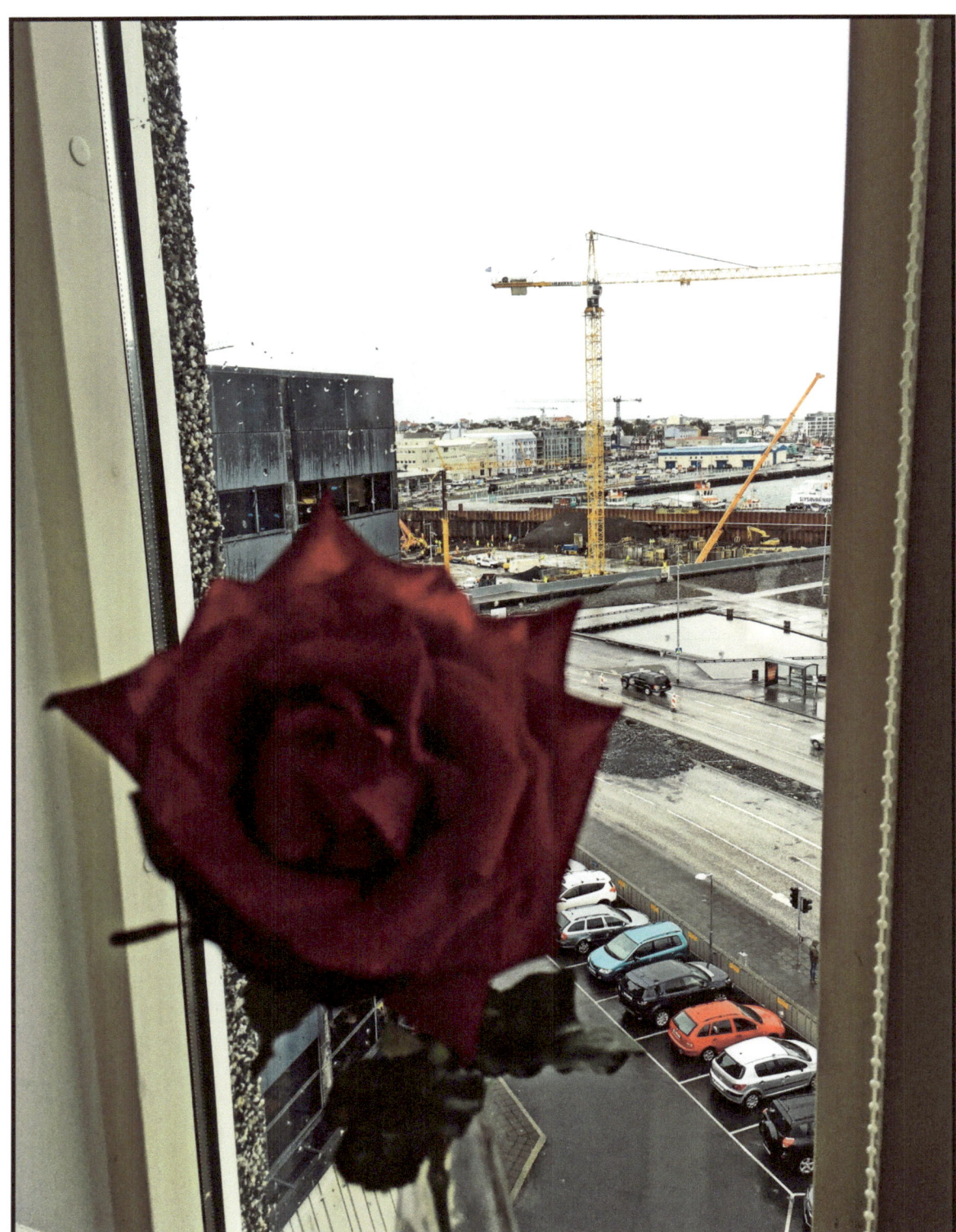

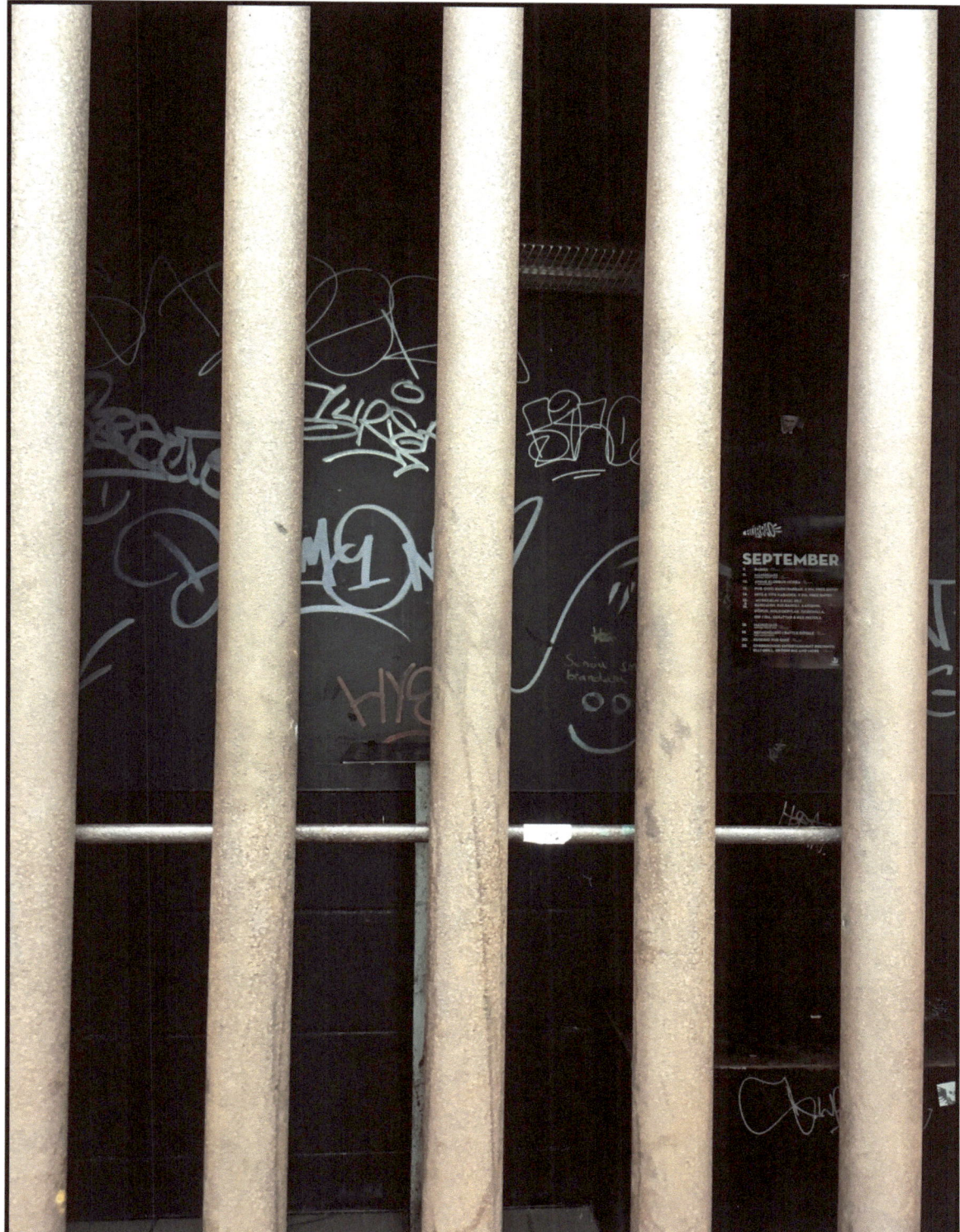

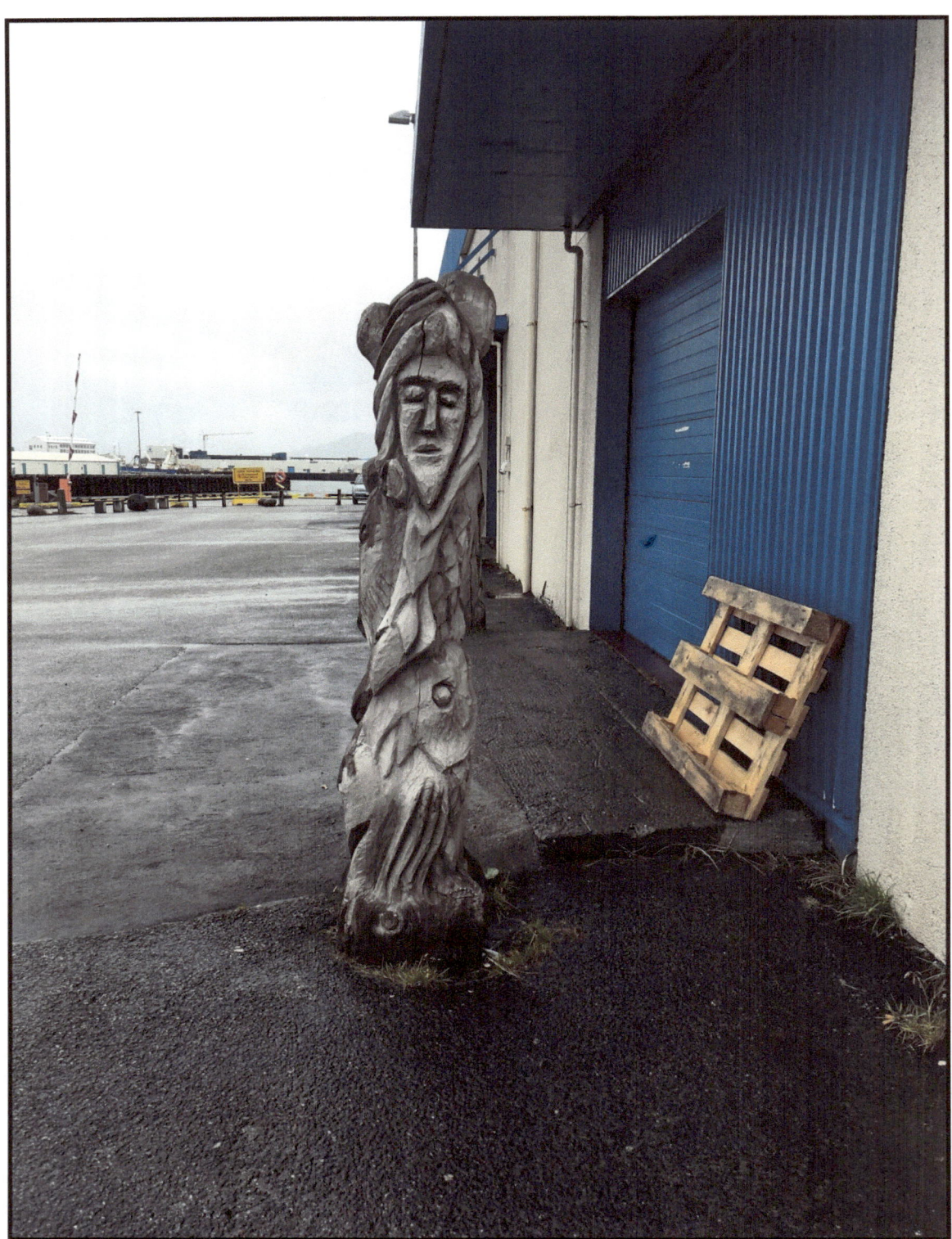

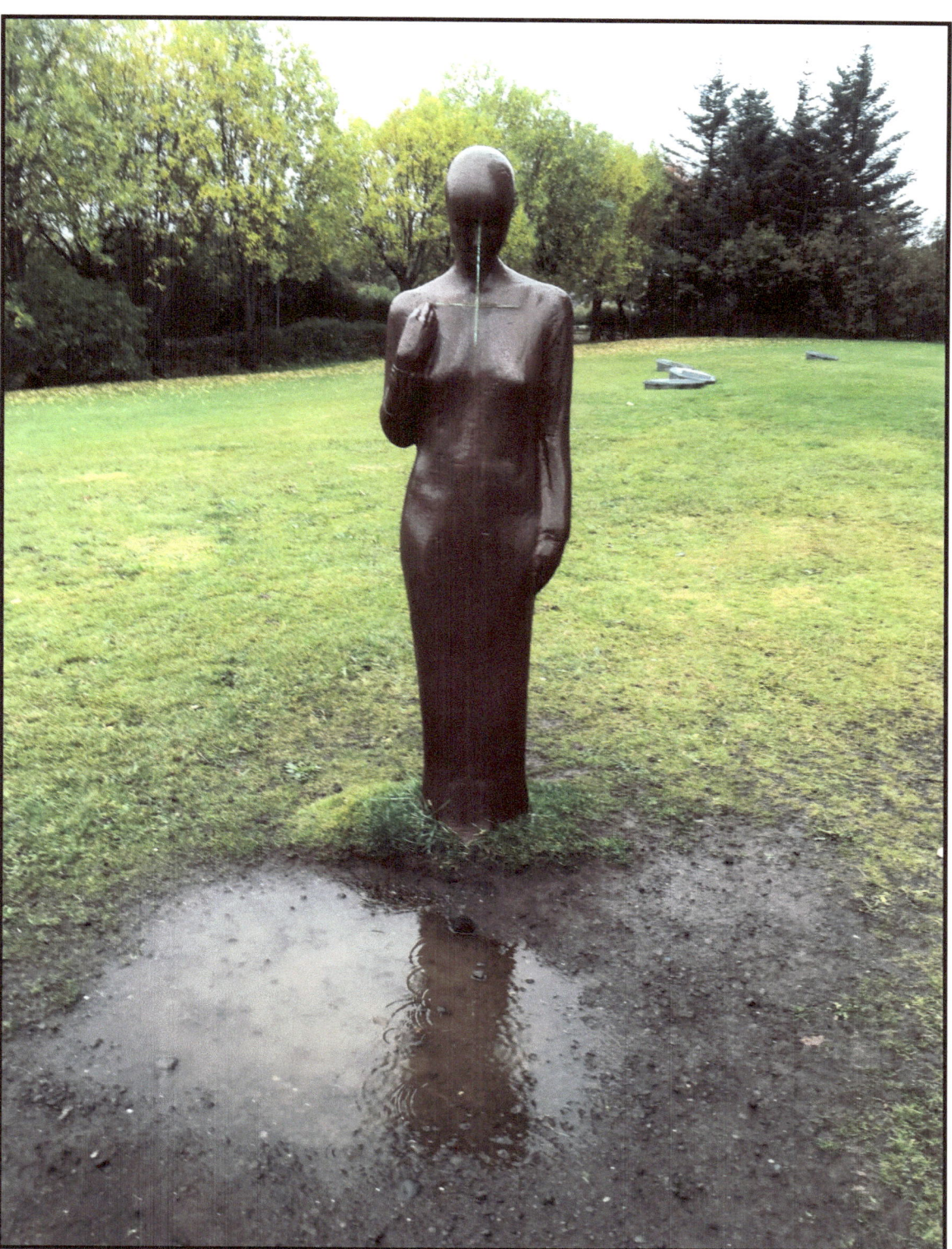

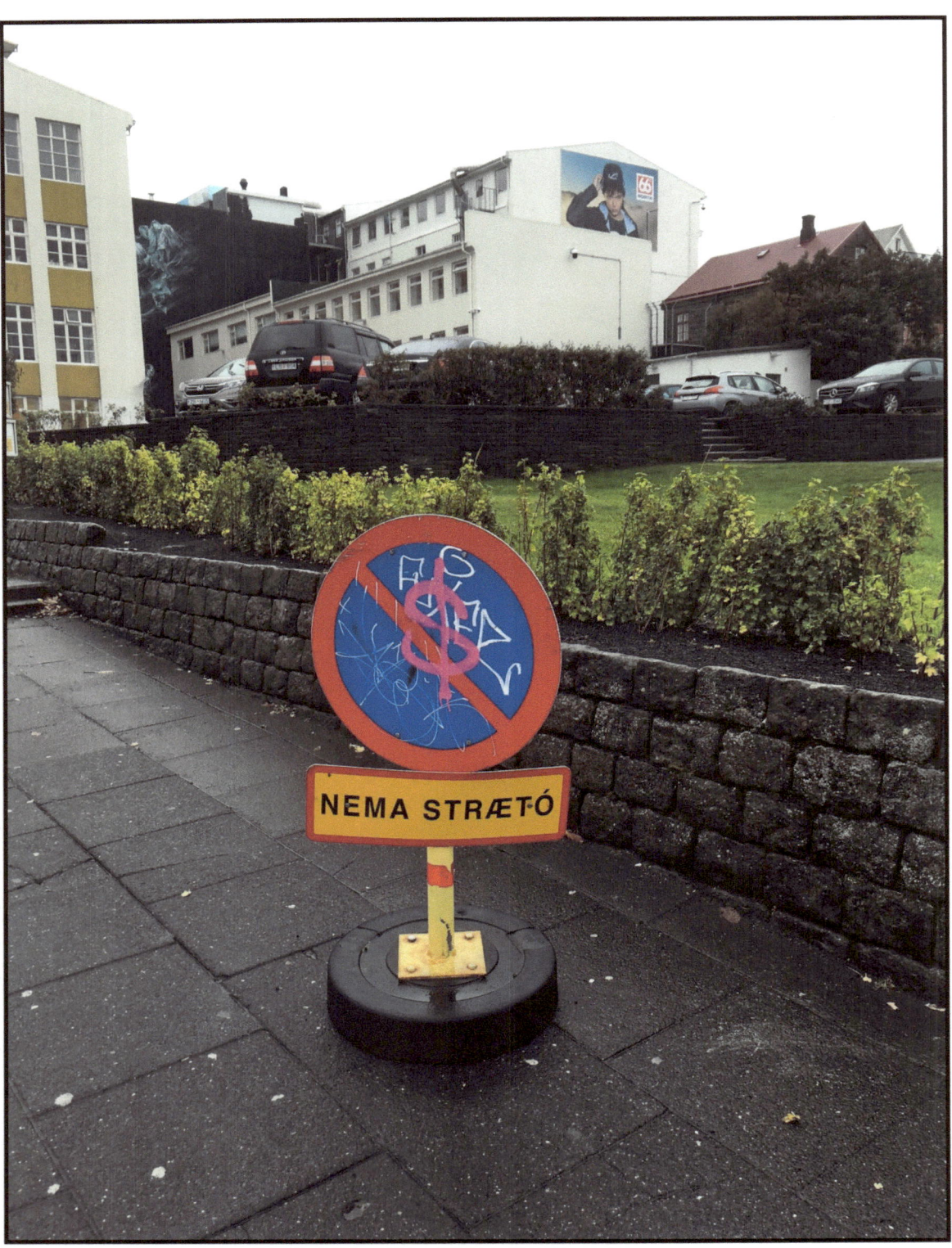

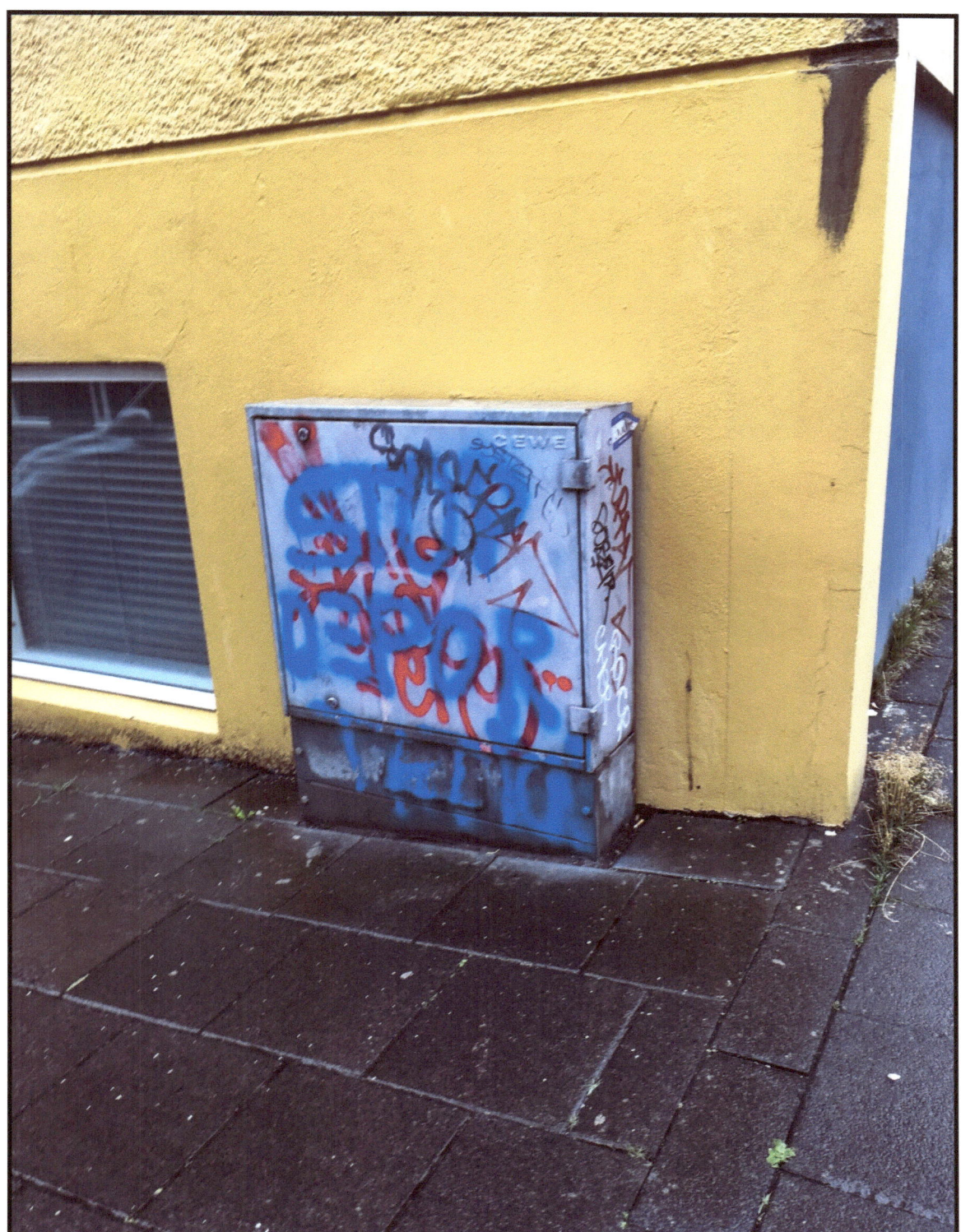

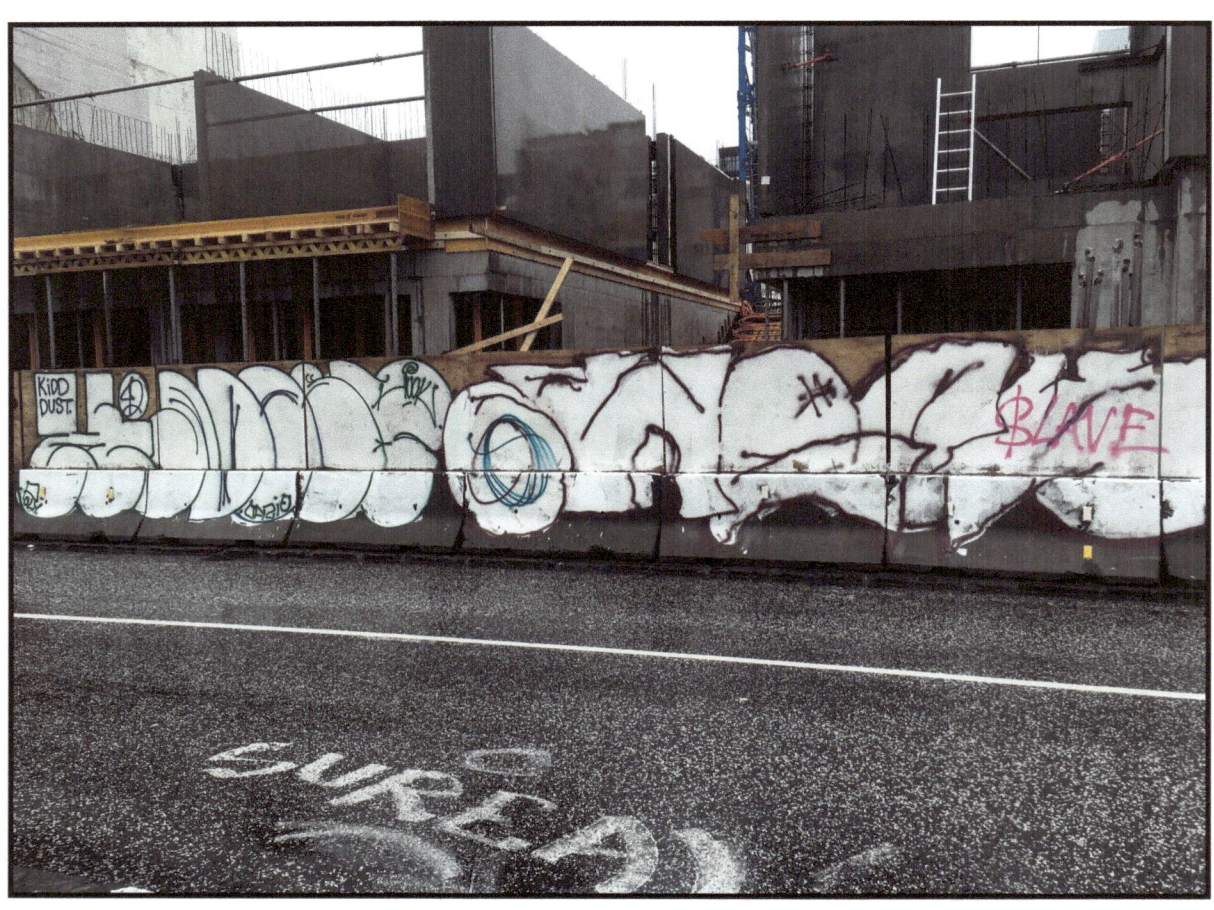

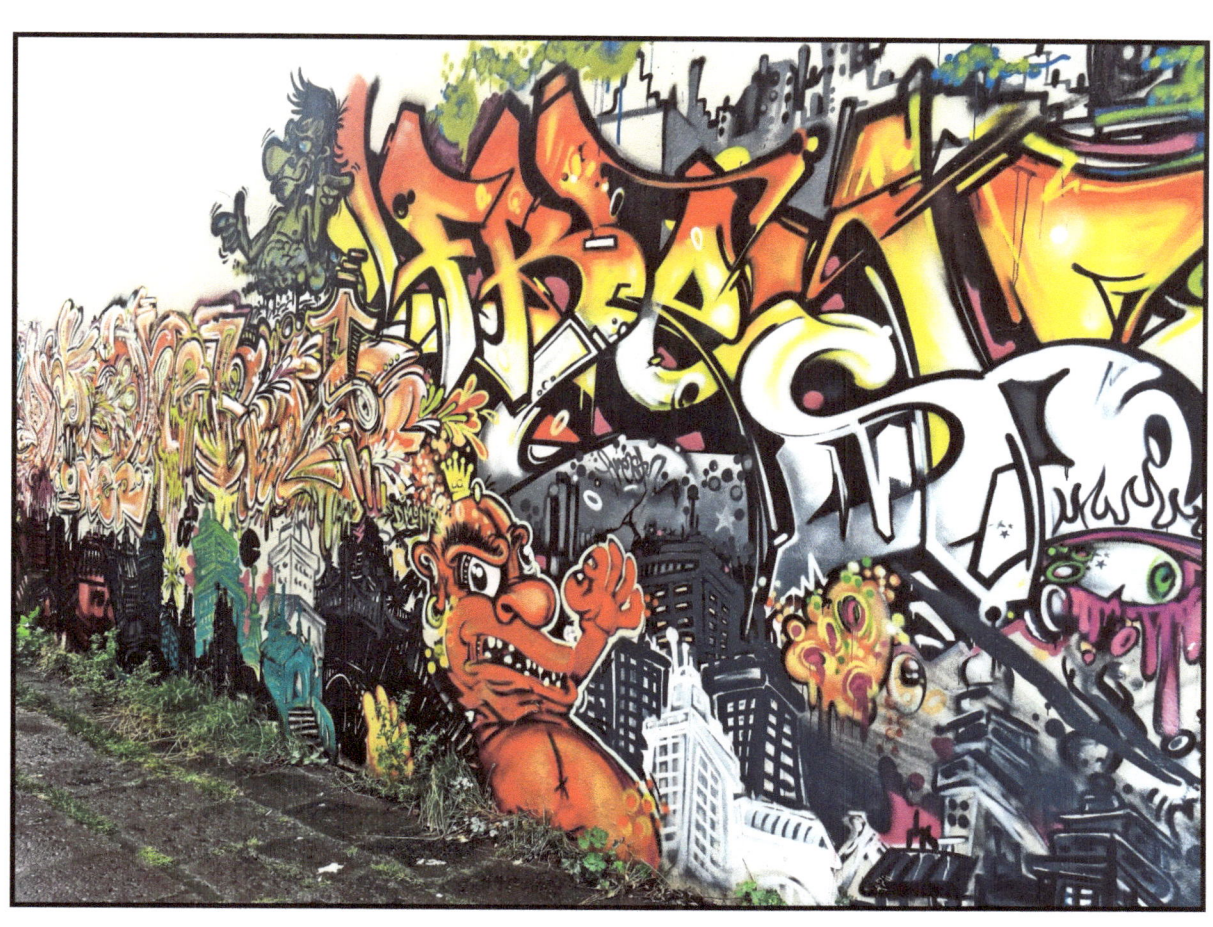

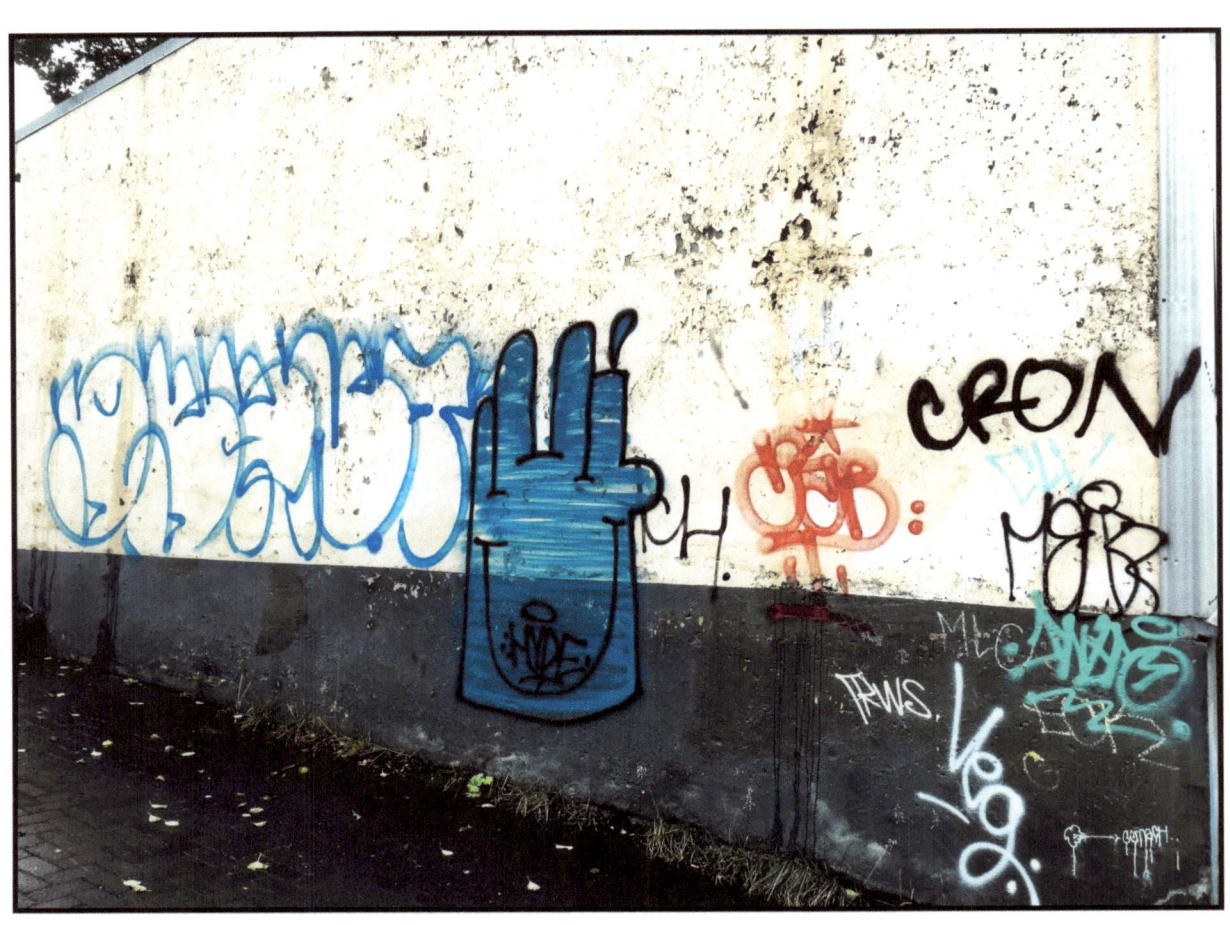

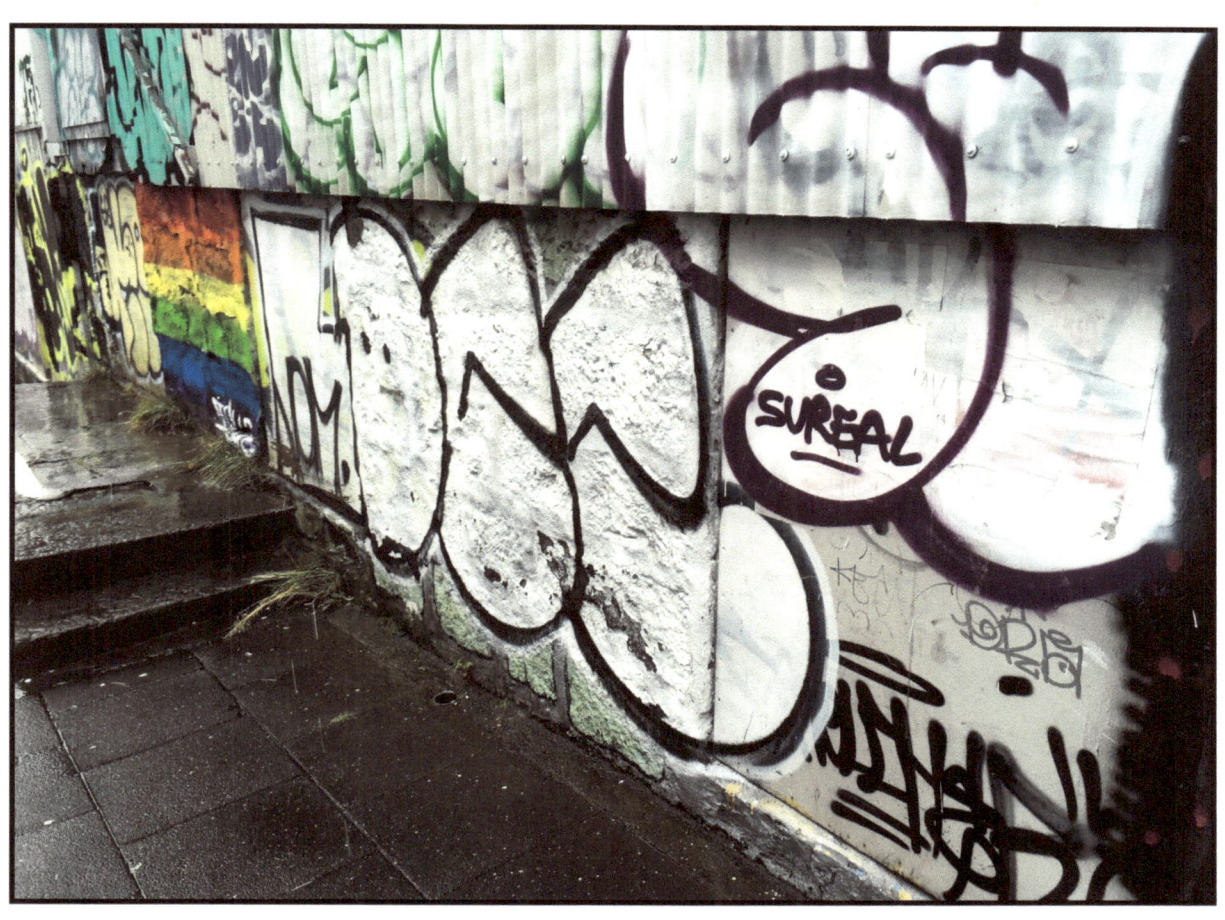

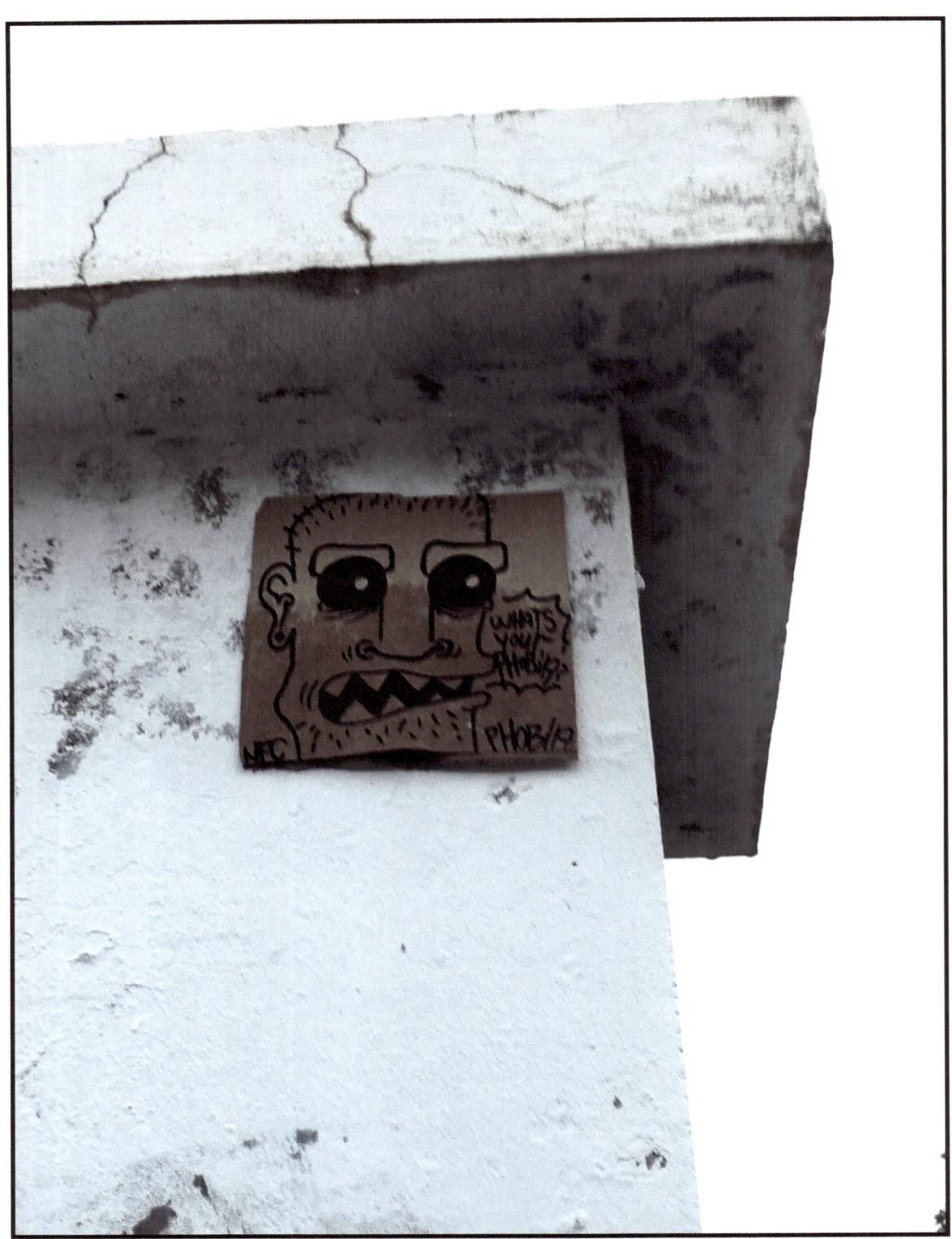

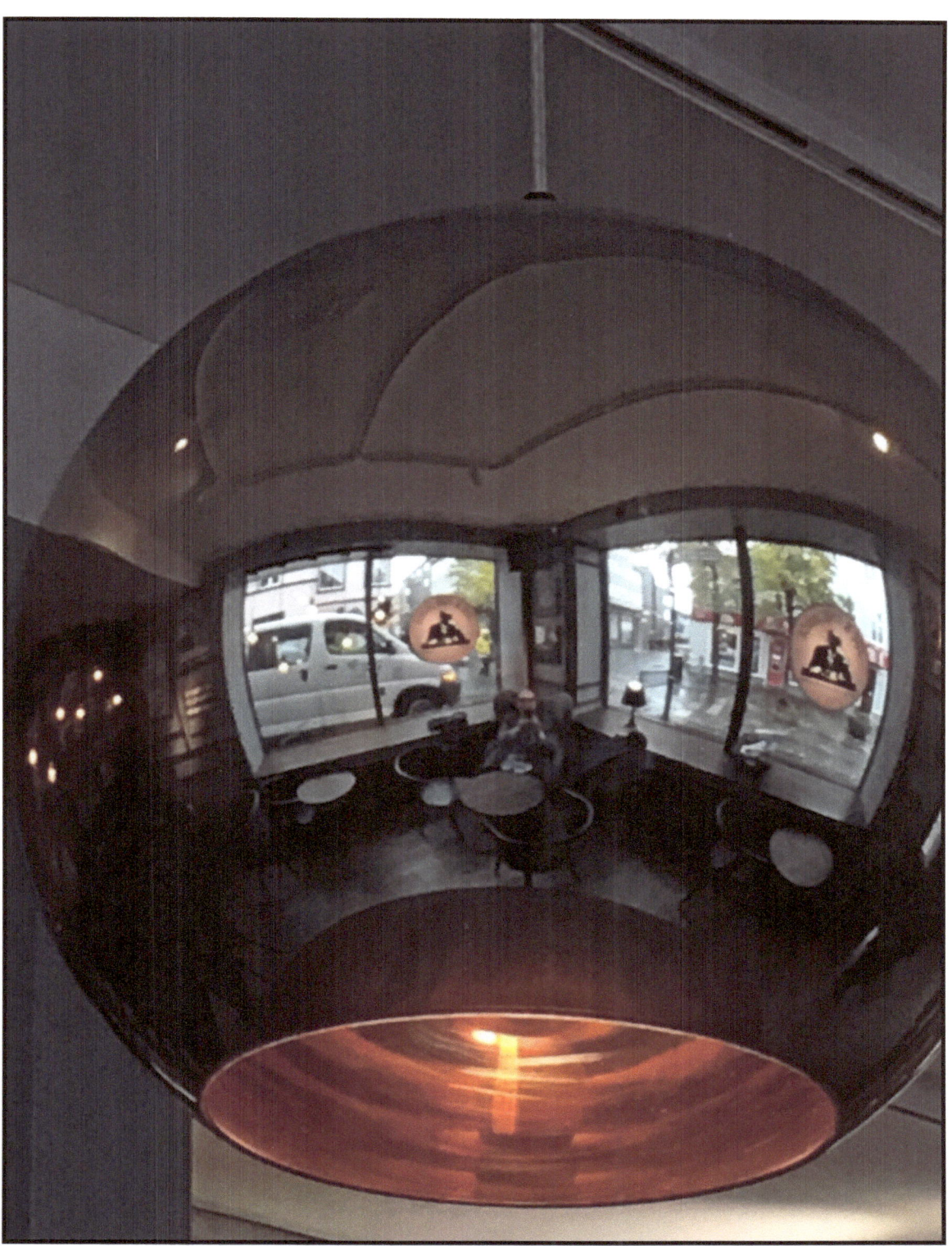

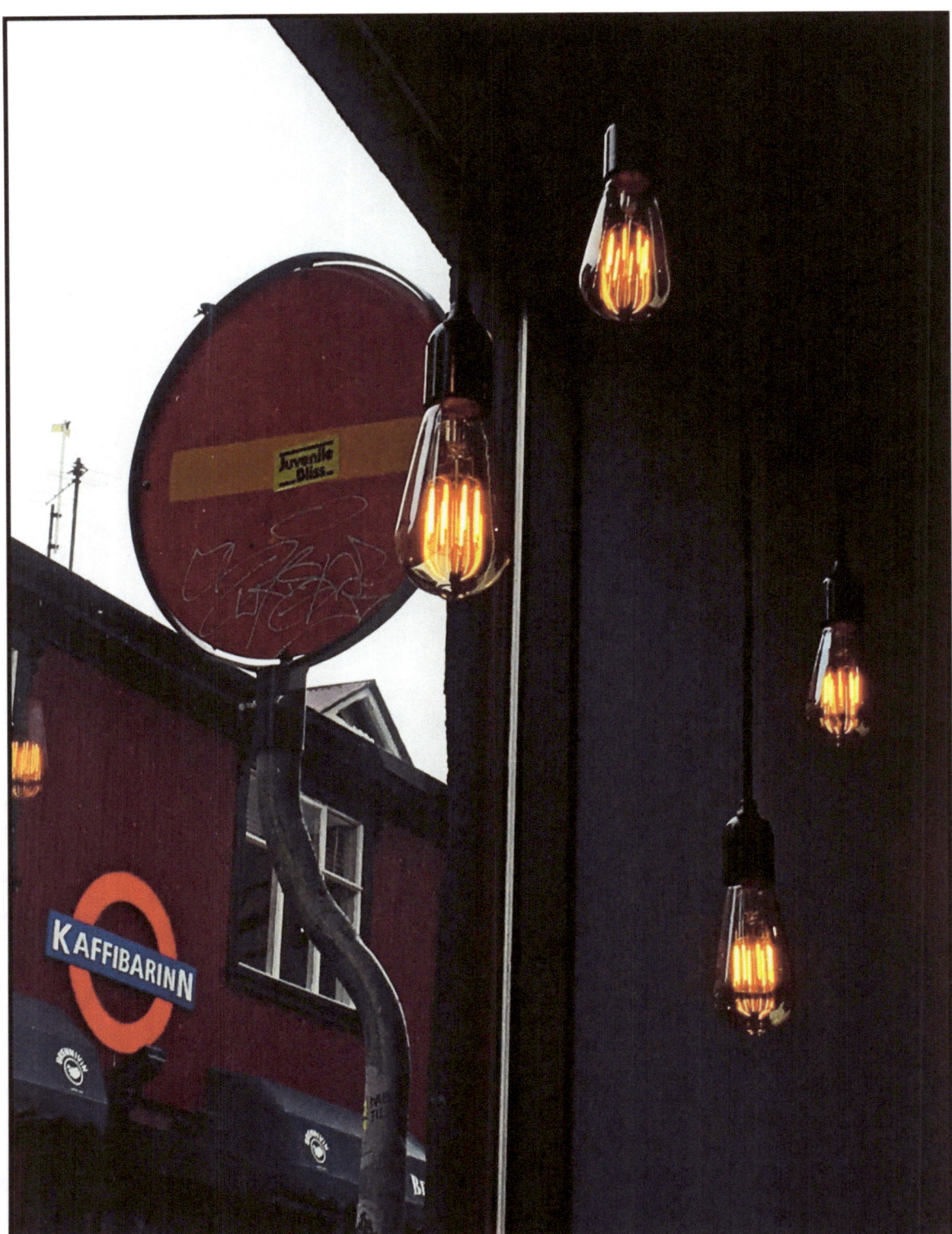

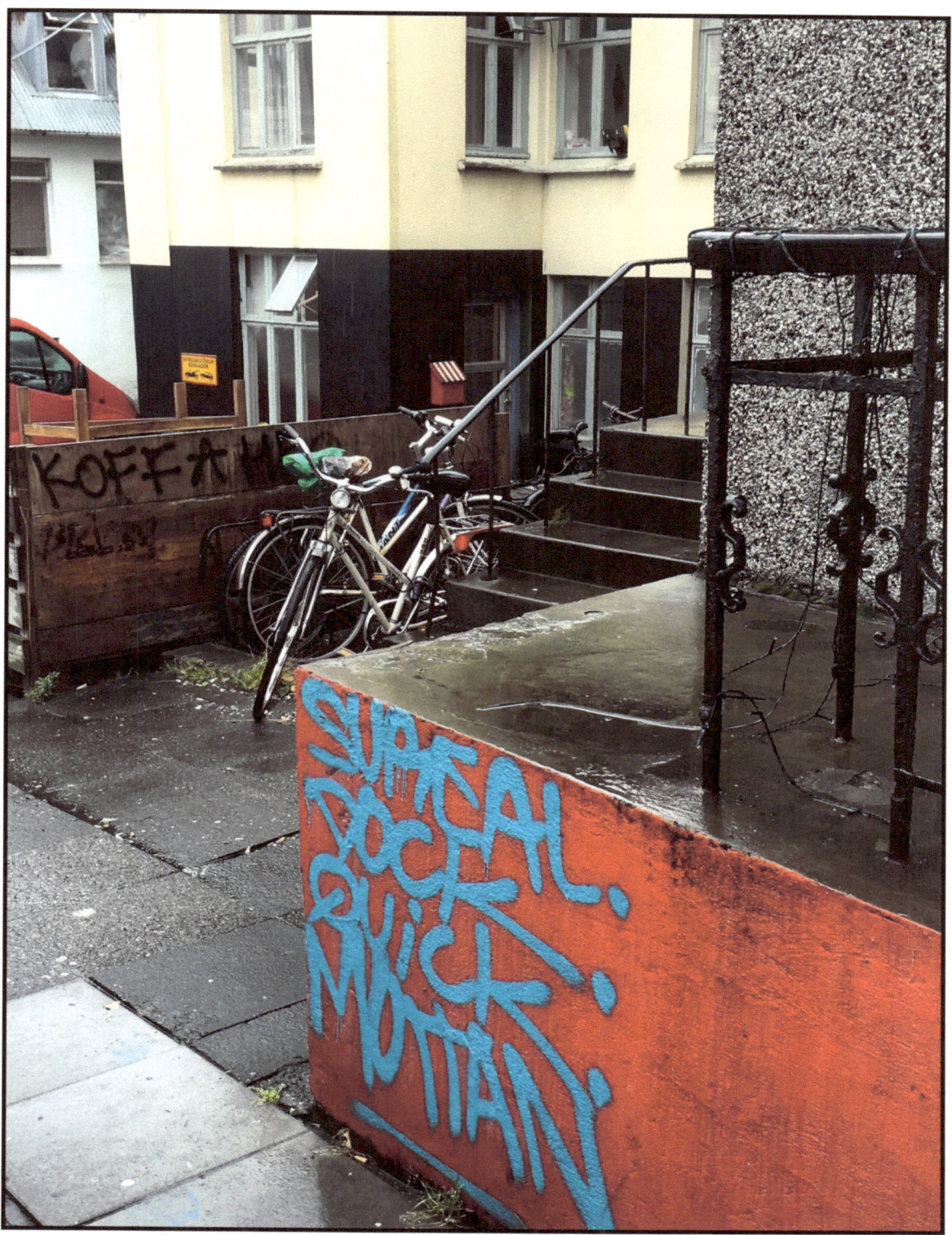

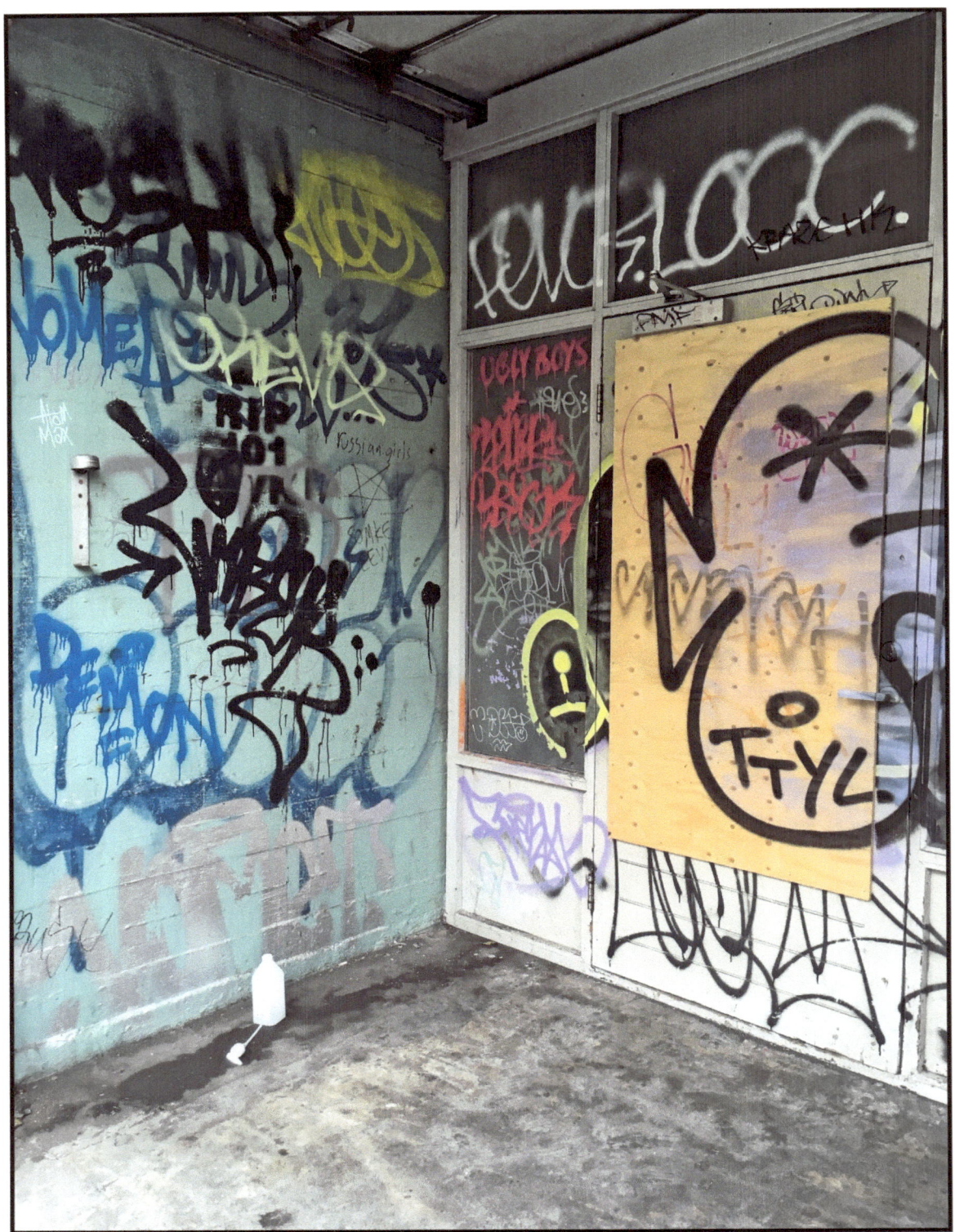

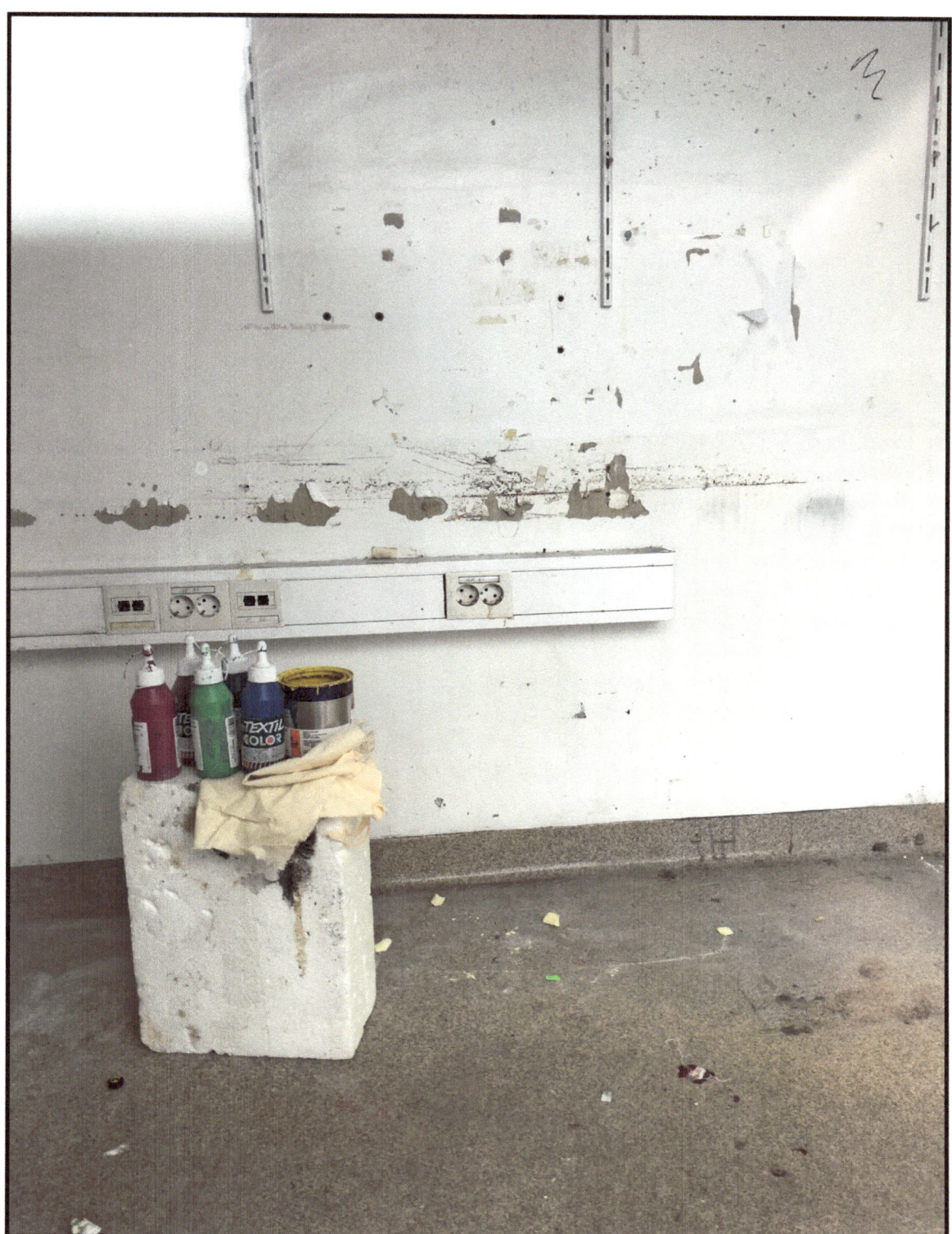

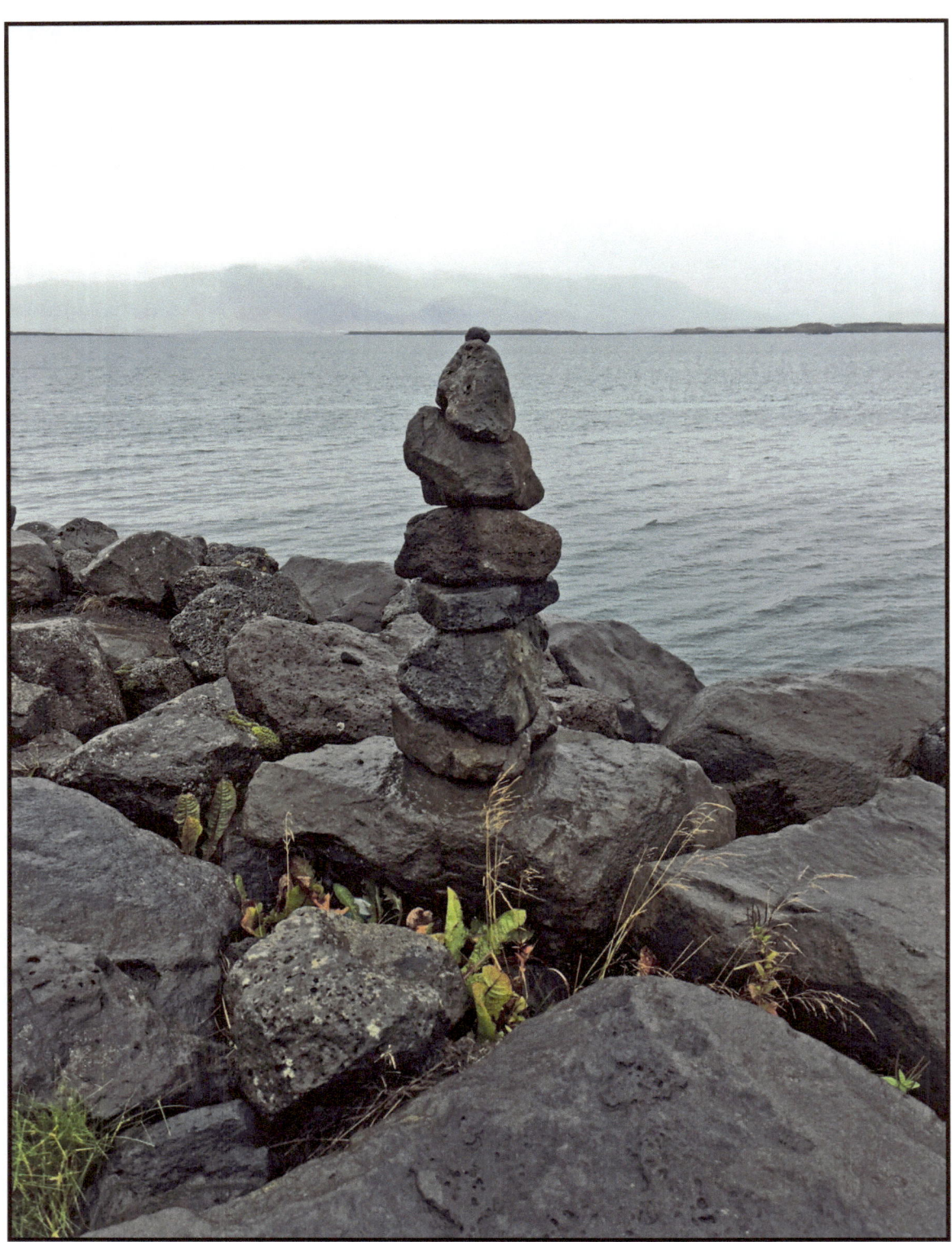

THE
ZEN